6 Years of Alaskan Adventures

D1108671

9-13-'93

To Molly Hart
Enjoy our adventures

by

Minerva C. Starritt

Minerva C. Starritt

Copyright © 1991 by Minerva C. Starritt.
All rights reserved.

Cover Sketch

*Earl Ohmer, "the shrimp king," and Eskimo
illustrations by Ralph F. Starritt*

Dedicated to
*My husband, Percy Starritt, without whom this story
would not have happened, and my friend, Elaine
McClellan, without whose gentle nagging it never
would have been written.*

Table of Contents

I. Getting Our Feet Wet

In April of 1936 I was teaching at Irving Creek School on the Klamath River. Valerie Beym (Lange) had the lower grades and I the upper.

Charles Graves, supervisor for the Indian children in the schools of California, came to see how Valerie and I were progressing and to inquire if he could help the Indian children in any of our projects. In the course of our conversation Mr. Graves said, "By the way, your friend Claude Hirst" (who had been Superintendent of Indian Education at Sacramento for the Bureau of Indian Affairs) "has been transferred to Alaska as Superintendent of Indian Education. Wouldn't you like to go to Alaska? I'm certain he would be pleased to have you as one of his teachers."

Claude owed me a favor. At Happy Camp the year previous, the Indian moms and dads wanted more Indian money for an athletic program. Claude refused their request. The parents became defiant, calling Claude names. That was when I stepped in and arranged a compromise. They received more money for the lunch program and a bit more for the athletic program. (Like the rest of us, Indians like to play, argue, and have fun.)

I had always wanted to go to Alaska. After school I went to T-Bar, where my husband, Perce, was working as a guard for the U.S. Forest Service. We temporarily occupied two tents there. One was filled with tools to fight fires and the other was our living quarters with a bed, stove, and orange crates instead of chests of drawers—a bit primitive. You should see the guard station at T-Bar today: lovely house, a building for tools and supplies, all the comforts of home.

We discussed Alaska and decided it would be a great

adventure. I wrote Claude at Juneau; my civil service papers came back at once, and I sent them to Washington D.C. Meanwhile, we finished building our log house at Orleans and moved in.

For several months I didn't hear a word; so I signed my contract for another year at the Irving Creek School with the understanding that I would be released if I heard from Alaska.

School started. On the last day of September a telegram arrived telling us to be at the Office of Indian Affairs in Seattle in one week to pick up my contract and our tickets. Our station would be Petersburg. What a scramble! I wired back that we would be there in two weeks. Now to get ready.

Perce's mother and father would take care of the log house, but what about my Chrysler convertible, my pride and joy? It was dark blue with a red leather interior and a rumble seat. That old car had hauled the baseball players to and from their games, up and down the Klamath River from Happy Camp to Willow Creek, as well as the children to play days at Hoopa, Somes Bar and other places. We had no buses in those days, only private transportation. What to do with the car? We needed money to make the trip and a little to get settled in Petersburg; so I would sell it. I was offered twenty-five dollars. That was ridiculous. Perce's brother Ed, who lived in Willow Creek, was an A-1 mechanic and had kept my car in perfect condition. I called Ed on the phone and said, "Would you like to have the car?" The answer was yes.

We picked Ed up at Willow Creek so that he could take us to Eureka to board a bus for Seattle. As we drove down the main street of Orleans, Perce's father was standing in front of the hotel waving good-bye. We knew we would not see him again. We didn't. Papa died of heart failure the following January.

In Seattle we picked up my contract and our tickets. On October fourth, we sailed aboard the *Northland*, a small freighter with a few cabins for passengers. We were treated like members of the crew and had the run of the boat. This was our first trip at sea. Across Queen Charlotte Sound, rough weather tossed us up and down and rolled us from side to side, but there was no sea sickness; we were good sailors.

Our first stop was Ketchikan. The early Tlingits, who lived there, had called the place *Shon*, which means creek. The Kitkatlans came to trap furs and added *Get*, meaning people. The whites came and put the two together, naming the place Ketchikan.

We walked through streets made of wooden planks, past carved cedar totem poles to a small bridge over the creek. The salmon were so thick you could walk across the stream on their backs.

Our next stop was Wrangell. Although we were there only an hour, I visited Chief Shake's Indian house. The building was about sixty feet wide and one hundred feet long. In each corner of the house was a post. I was told a live slave had been put in the ground and the post put on top of him for good luck. (I would have had bad dreams sleeping in that house.) Shakes—slabs of cedar bark—formed the roof, held down by rocks. There was a smoke hole with a shutter which could be shifted, according to the direction of the wind. A platform about six feet wide ran around the four sides of the building. It was divided into sections for the several families that lived in the house. There were as many as thirty or forty people living in one house. In the middle of the earthen floor burned a fire, where the cooking for all the families was done. The totem pole, which is like a coat of arms or the history of the clan, stood in front of the house.

Chief Shake's totem was the young raven, Yethl. According to legend, Yethl was responsible for bringing fire, the sun, moon and stars to mankind. When the chief died in 1916, his widow kept the house and most of the family heirlooms on display as a tourist attraction.

When we returned to the boat the officers gave us a farewell party. About 2:00 a.m., after a dizzying number of toasts, we arrived on the dock at Petersburg. Returning the officers' waves and shouted good wishes, we nearly ran into a tall, raincoated woman, who was holding an umbrella and looking exceedingly proper. The supervisor from Juneau had come to meet us! She raised no eyebrow at our exuberance but welcomed us warmly.

The three of us picked up the luggage, which consisted of two duffle bags and a suitcase. We traveled light in the North. Except for our personal belongings, everything we needed would be furnished. On a street made of planks, we walked two blocks to the hotel. As the clerk conducted us up the stairs, we met an Indian woman complacently putting a large roll of bills in her purse. At two o'clock in the morning? Ah, well, we were in Alaska.

The next day I got my first look at Petersburg. Petersburg is on a long spit extending out into the narrows with high, snowcapped mountains in the background. It is a Norwegian town situated on the tip of Mitkof Island. The first settlers, who had come in the Gold Rush days to mine, were forced ashore at Frederick Sound. Finding fishing profitable, they named the town after one of their members and sent for their families.

On the main street were the hotel, a liquor store, the bank (the richest per capita in America), and the trading post, which handled hardware, groceries, rain gear and work clothes. (It rains every day in southeastern Alaska.) Then there was Miss Cornelius' drygoods store. She carried dresses and shoes. She also made the best butter cookies you ever tasted. We later became close friends because I needed someone to talk to and she was a good listener. Across the street was the cold storage plant where the halibut boats iced the fish before heading for Prince Rupert or Seattle. There was a second street of just beer and wine joints. They were busy places, teeming with natives and fishermen. From the hotel window, I could see the long dock and the shrimp cannery belonging to Earl Ohmer. Tied there were ten or twelve shrimp boats with their large nets. The nets would scrape the bottom of the sea and come back loaded with small shrimp and some large spider (or king) crab.

The next morning we moved to the Indian School, an old two story wooden building two blocks up the hill from the main street. Downstairs were a large classroom with a tall pot-bellied stove, a room full of powdered coal, and the government nurse's quarters, which consisted of one private room plus a bathroom shared with the school children. When we arrived, the nurse, Miss Weightman, was in Wrangell. Our living quarters were upstairs: living room, bathroom, bedroom, and kitchen. Off the bedroom was a large closet, full of surplus canned beef. That canned beef was the best I have ever eaten. It helped our budget, believe me!

The next day, Sunday, we heard a knock at the door. Our neighbor from across the street, Earl Ohmer, "The Shrimp King," had come to present us with a large spider crab and welcome us to Petersburg.

"Any time, come to the cannery and help yourself to crab and shrimp at no charge," he invited. Earl wore large horn-rimmed glasses, had a bushy mustache and a well-trimmed beard, smoked a pipe, wore a wide-brimmed dark hat, a fancy beaded Indian vest with an old fashioned watch fob in his pocket, knee breeches and spats. He was a bit of a showman, but what a wonderful guy he was, with a heart as big as all outdoors. Most of his employees were Tlingit Indians, and we worked together to assist them with their problems.

How the shrimp cannery did stink! The first time I went to the cannery, I wore a wool coat. I didn't know any better. The shrimp odor saturated the wool; dry cleaning did not help. I burned the coat. You had to wear slickers in the cannery. In autumn, people put shrimp pickings on their lawns; a wonderful fertilizer, but then the whole town smelled of shrimp.

Early Monday morning I stoked that pot-bellied stove with powdered coal. Twenty-two children arrived, all shapes and sizes in all eight grades. A week later I had only seven: two Pickernals, four Baileys, and Alan Williams, my single first grader. The salmon fishing had ended and the other families had traveled westward to their villages— Kake, Hoonah, and Klawack.

By the end of the second week, Miss Weightman arrived. What wonderful memories I have of her! She took me under her wing, and I began to learn in depth about the community and my pupils. Petersburg had a large Territorial School where the Indian children were not welcome, especially the Pickernals and the Baileys. This was understandable, since we had to delouse them every morning before school.

The Pickernals and Baileys were related and lived in shanties along the waterfront. Miss Weightman and I visited them often in an attempt to persuade them to be cleaner and to stop drinking—the father, Ben Bailey, especially. He was the best totem carver in Petersburg, when he was sober. He carved only when in jail. I managed to keep Ben in jail a good deal after the deputy marshall and I became friends. The deputy owed me favors because, at 300 lbs., he was too fat to drive his car. I was deputized and drove when he had to arrest a woman. In return he would keep Ben in jail as long as possible, which was a good part of the time; so Ben could carve, thus supporting his family from the sale of totem poles.

Alan Williams was my pride and joy. His mother worked for Earl Ohmer, "The Shrimp King," in the cannery. She was a widow; Alan was her only child. He was smart, clean, and happy. I would keep him until his mother got off work and sometimes all night when she worked the midnight shift. He was like my own little boy. He loved to dress in his cowboy suit with his big hat, especially when I took him shopping and to see Ben at the jail.

About the third week of school, the weather turned very cold. We banked the potbelled stove at night: that was a mistake. That Alaskan coal acted like gunpowder. About midnight the top of the stove blew off with a loud explosion. I thought someone had thrown a bomb. We ran downstairs. Soot covered everything! I couldn't hold school in that mess. Margaret (Miss Weightman), Perce and I cleaned all next day. That did it! I went to the trading post and ordered an oil stove, tank, and fifty gallons of oil without authorization. When my boss received the bills, he almost fired me. I did get a big lecture: the Government likes its paperwork.

Perce found work on the dredge. Frederick Sound was being deepened for large boats. The dirt was put on barges two hundred feet long, then hauled out to sea. This was a dangerous trip in rough weather; men had been washed overboard. So when the wind roared, the dirt was taken to Scow Bay fourteen miles away, where the men would stay all night.

After the dredging was finished Perce found work at

the Swenson Brothers Mill across the bay. There he met Jess Ames who owned a mink ranch; so he went to work for Jess.

The mink ranch provided a different kind of occupation and was interesting. There were long mink sheds with each animal in a separate cage. Mink are very nervous and need to be watched, especially after having their litters; the mother might eat her young. A special formula of scrap fish, trout, eggs, and vitamins was fed to the three hundred mink. Fishing, feeding, and caring for those little animals occupied Jess, Perce, and a third employee, Ed Young. Ed had captured two land otters, a male and a female. He could take the otters and some of the mink out of their cages without being bitten, which was unusual. He played games with the otters, but to his disappointment they never mated in captivity.

After two months, we knew few people socially. I wondered about that. Of course there were Earl, Miss Cornelius, Ed Locken, the banker, the Ameses, Ed the Marshal, and the two Salvation Army "girls" who lived across the street. Perce had some men friends—rather, drinking pals—he had worked with on the dredge. I mentioned this isolation to Margaret. She said the teacher at the Indian School was, like the Indians, not accepted by white society. I decided to do something about that.

In my younger days, I liked to sing. My voice was fair; I could carry a tune; so I decided to go to the main church in Petersburg and sing in the choir. That was an excellent decision. Now accepted socially, we made many wonderful friends like Dr. Rude, his wife Amy, the Stedmans, the Rustads and Bue Hentze, a small man who loved to polka. How he and I jumped around on the dance floor!

Christmas was approaching. The Salvation Army women and the Indians attended the community church. They asked me to arrange and direct a Christmas program. I accepted. The two women, my students, and the church-going Indians would help. A young Indian woman was the pianist. She was an excellent musician, but I had to drag her out of the beer joint every time we had a practice. She was laughing all the time I pulled her along. I thought, what will happen on Christmas Eve? Surprisingly she was on time. I even sang a solo, "O Holy Night." I was frightened, but I made it through the song with help from an Indian man with a fine voice. Since that time I have had great respect for the Salvation Army and their work and for my many Indian friends with their sense of humor. By February I was convinced that it would be a waste of money and time to repair and retain the old rundown Indian School for seven children: this didn't make sense. I told Claude how I felt about the school. By coincidence, the head of Indian Education in the United States and the Territory was visiting Alaska. Claude told me to have all my data ready to show him that the school was not needed. The data was ready and my speech was too. Borrowing Dr. Rude's car, I picked up Claude and his boss at the dock. They had only one half hour to decide the fate of the Petersburg Indian School before the boat sailed. It was enough time. The school was to be closed.

Claude asked, "Where do you want to go in Alaska?" I replied, "We came to see the North, not to be in a place like Petersburg or southeastern Alaska. This is like being in Puget Sound."

He really took me at my word, and on May 17, 1937, I received the following letter:

"As a result of the present reorganization of positions and personnel of the Alaska School Service, a number of changes will naturally follow. In each case where employees are affected, we are notifying them to that effect.

"This is to advise that we are recommending your transfers as Community Workers grade 9, at $2,000 and $2,040 per annum to Kotlik (Chaneliak) as teachers in the Community School effective not prior to September 1, 1937. The usual deductions of $240 per annum for living quarters will also be made, if furnished by the Government in accordance with regulations. You will be able to travel on the *North Star*, the Government boat, to St. Michael where you will board a smaller local boat to reach Chaneliak.

"Chaneliak is a small, one-teacher station where you will find the work in many ways more satisfying than that at Petersburg. Everyone who has worked with Eskimos always speaks most enthusiastically about them.

"It is not likely that we will know what action the Washington Office will take until in July or later, so you should take no definite steps until you hear further from this office.

"Yours very truly, Chas. W. Hawkesworth, Assistant to Director."

Meanwhile, when school closed in June, I was sent as matron to Wrangell Institute, a large government high school, boarding students from all lower Alaska. My charges were six girls who were spending the summer at school in order to accept employment in the salmon cannery. They were also to do their own cooking and work in the laundry that served a small hospital on campus, where students with tuberculosis were treated. The laundry was huge, with large boilers, great steam presses, enormous tubs, and oversized washing machines. Staring at that set-up in amazement, I concluded that somehow I had wandered into the wrong profession; but I managed.

The Cassadys, who had been teaching several years at Wrangell, were leaving in August with their five-year-old son. They had asked me to dinner not knowing the boy had been exposed to the mumps.

Two weeks later, I dragged myself awake one morning with an aching head. Looking at my swollen face in the mirror, I diagnosed—mumps! I toiled upstairs in the staff house to report my problem to the superintendent, a nervous little man. When he saw me, he slammed the door in my face, screaming, "Go downstairs to your apartment." I had to laugh, but that hurt. Mrs. Cassady felt responsible and brought me soup every day. Fortunately, my mumps were a light case and I was back at work in a few days.

The Institute owned a large launch with four cabins. One Saturday the superintendent decided that before the Cassadys and I left, we would take the school girls on a two day trip through the inlets. I thought it would be nice to have ice cream. I made it with powdered eggs. It was the most terrible stuff you ever tasted. We threw it overboard.

As we sailed along the inlet, we saw a mother bear with twin cubs catching salmon. The cubs were playing instead of learning their lesson: so Mama Bear gave them a good cuff on the ears. Further on, a curious blue fox ran along the beach watching us. Tall spruce trees and ferns were growing on the edge of the banks. What an enjoyable way to end six weeks at Wrangell Institute!

Perce had been out on one of the islands working for McDonald, falling timber and rafting logs to Juneau. Having fallen off a raft and hurt his knee, he had returned to Petersburg. When I arrived there from Wrangell, there was a letter telling us to be ready to board the *North Star* on August the thirteenth. Arrangements with the Seattle office had already been made at the Bank of Petersburg to pay for our year's supply of groceries, which would be transported on the *North Star*. Did you ever try to figure out what you eat for three hundred and sixty-five days? What a challenge! We ordered too much cereal, rice, flour, corn meal, gum drops, and everything else.

By chance, Margaret Weightman was at Petersburg. We promised to write. Little did I know how much I would need her advice and help after we arrived at Chaneliak.

On August thirteenth at 5:00 p.m. the *U.S.M.D. North Star*, the ship of the Bureau of Indian Affairs, sailed majestically into Frederick Sound. This was the same ship Admiral Byrd had used when he discovered the South Pole. Captain S.T.L. Whitlam of the *North Star* had designed the ship. He had piloted for many years through the Bering Strait before designing this vessel and knew what was needed. The bow was rounded like a belly and reinforced with special thick steel plates so that it could ride up on the ice floes, crushing some of the ice at the same time. The ship could then back off without any damage. It had two portholes at the top of the bow giving it a strange appearance, like a great monster looking at you.

Standing on Citizens Dock waiting, were Mr. McDonald, enroute to Juneau to see about his logs; John Jacob Jackson, a deaf mute bound for school at Juneau, Perce, and I.

To our great surprise, the ship went sailing past us to anchor in the channel a mile away. The launch was sent in for us. Here I was, all dressed up in my best bib and tucker, wearing a new fur coat Perce had just bought for me. Did you ever climb a rope ladder on the side of a ship? It swings from side to side. I was more than a bit frightened but made it to the top where an officer helped me aboard. That was the last time I wore a dress to board a ship: slacks and ski pants were for me!

We had another surprise. After anticipating an enjoyable sea voyage together, Perce and I were separated. The men had to go to steerage. Women shared the staterooms. I was lodged with three other women, Mrs. Benawa going to Galowin, Katherine McMillan going to Noatak, and Clarice Kerr, a nurse bound for Point Barrow. Clarice was the largest woman I had ever known and the jolliest.

Clarice and two other nurses, Alma Carlson and Miss Keaton, were called the warhorses of the North. They were strong women, had their own dog teams and traveled alone from village to village helping the Eskimos. Carlson took care of the Eskimos on the lower Yukon and the Kuskokwin Rivers, Keaton on the Seward Peninsula and Noatak River, and Kerr served at Point Hope, Point Barrow and the top of Alaska.

Stopping at Juneau where many passengers embarked, Perce and I went through a driving rainstorm to the Office of Indian Affairs. Perce signed an agreement to work for the government and the Forest Service and to oversee the herds of reindeer in our territory.

Back on the ship and on our way to Seward, Perce and the other men decided they would not sleep in the steerage any longer. They had a sit-down strike and slept in the social hall for three nights. Perce, McMillan, Connelly, and Thomas agitated until they had the entire crew and all the passengers helping them in their cause.

Sigfried Sundt, Chief Steward, figured he was outnumbered and made arrangements for the men to have staterooms with their wives and children. It was to be a wonderful and memorable cruise.

Approaching Seward, we saw high, snow-capped mountains in the background and a picturesque bay, a beautiful setting for the city. There were rough seas as we crossed the gulf, but Perce and I were good sailors, no jumpy stomachs. We sailed serenely into Resurrection Bay and tied up at Seward. Here the crew had to unpack the hold because the supplies had been loaded backwards in Seattle. Freight for Point Barrow and Point Hope was on the top. Supplies to be shipped by rail from Seward to the stations in the interior were on the bottom. In the confusion, some of our freight was put on the railroad. We didn't know this until later.

Because of the delay, we were able to get better acquainted with the passengers and, especially, with the officers. The galley was at our disposal: great food and plenty of it. We were like a big family on holiday. Before leaving Seward, we were joined by Evelyn I. Butler, our supervisor. Dr. Butler was traveling among her various schools and would spend the greater part of the winter in the west and north.

After leaving Seward, we had pleasant sailing until a storm blew up. The ship tossed up and down and from side to side; if you went on deck you had to hold the ropes or railing. We were told to stay in our cabins. I ventured out but soon went back to the cabin holding the rope all the way lest I be thrown overboard.

Later, in calmer seas, we saw whales shooting water high in the air. Along the Aleutians we saw the volcano Pavlof puffing great volumes of smoke and fire. What a sight! It was like being in fairyland, sailing smoothly along. Geologists told us that islands will appear and disappear along the Aleutians—"The Islands of a Thousand Smokes."

We could smell the whaling station as we approached Akutan, where we docked to leave supplies for the school before sailing into the Bering Sea. At midnight, on the dock, men were cutting up a huge whale. With all its stink we couldn't sleep; so we disembarked and walked through the mess of blood and guts to the end of the path away from the smell, past the cookhouse, sleeping quarters and hospital. The moon was just coming up over that small sheltered bay casting light and shadows on the water. Hearing the ship's horn, a signal for us to return, we hurried back and sailed out of the bay into the fog.

We anchored in the fog. Why? Maybe because Chief Officer Bush wanted to call a meeting of the knitters', crocheters', darners', and sewers', associations of which he was the slave driver. You see, I had been trying to teach Clarice to knit Red Cross spiral socks. She was knitting too loose and they were as big as gunny sacks. She wanted to give them to Bush. Charles, the second officer, a big tease, knew Clarice could never get the socks to fit, but in the meantime I was knitting a pair that would fit for Clarice to give to Bush.

After raising anchor we moved slowly through thick fog. We anchored off Nelson Island at 9:30 p.m. Bush and Charles were loading the barge and launch, getting ready to go ashore with supplies for the teachers on Nelson Island. Clarice and I were knitting frantically. Clarice bet Charles five dollars that she would finish Bush's socks by the time they returned. About 2:00 a.m. we could hear the launch returning. The socks that fit were finished: we ran to the rail waving them. We had the last laugh on those two teases and the five dollars to boot!

We were getting close to the Arctic Circle. I went top side to the pilot house to talk to Captain Whitlam. Curious about what we would find at our destination, I asked him what an Eskimo village was like. Smiling, he answered, "Dirt, kids, and dogs, and I hope you have plenty of gum for the kids." How right he was!

We had a masquerade party the night we crossed the Arctic Circle. Passengers and crew decorated the social hall. Everyone had to be in costume and wear a mask. Clarice and I made up most of the passengers in our stateroom. We dressed Perce as a call girl in Clarice's pink lace nightgown. He made a beautiful woman, believe it or not. We started to make up Clarice. We were tying two pillows on her front and back, when Bush rushed into the cabin to deliver his uniform for me to wear. He burst out laughing holding his stomach; of course we all joined him. Clarice looked so funny with a red bandanna on her head while we were pinning a red tablecloth around her waist for a skirt. She was as big as a house. Bush was afraid she wouldn't get through the cabin door but she made it by turning sideways. Mrs. Benawa wore the captain's suit. She looked like a midget.

When we got to the social hall, Perce began kissing the officers and men, much to their disgust. He caused quite a stir, smearing lipstick on all of them. No one recognized him until he took off his mask. One of the crew played the piano and we all sang. Stuart Widener and I did a tap dance. It was Officer Charles' birthday, but he didn't appear. I think he was afraid to show up because he had played so many tricks on everyone. We had a jolly good time: it would be one of our last nights together, since we were to dock at Nome the next day. Then we would go on to Saint Michael where we would embark on the last leg of our journey.

By 8:00 a.m. we had eaten breakfast and were ready for sight seeing in Nome. The *North Star* dropped anchor. The Coast Guard launch came to the ship with the Government teacher and a male passenger, the husband of our traveling companion Mrs. Nylund. "Honey, Honey, Honey," we had heard all through the journey; so we all had a good look at Honey. He was like jolly Old Saint Nick. You couldn't help liking him and we understood why we had heard "Honey, Honey, Honey" the entire trip.

Because of the shallow water, everything had to be lightered off the ship, both freight and passengers. Clarise, Evelyn Butler, Mrs. Benawa and I got on the freight platform where we held to the ropes at the four corners. Charles was at the winch. He raised us up over the Bering Sea and began to swing the platform back and forth. We hung on to the ropes for dear life. Clarise and I were yelling at him to stop, Evelyn was a bit angry and little Mrs. Benawa was very frightened. Finally he lowered us to the Goast Guard launch. We wanted to get even with Charles for giving us a scare but everyone watching was laughing, thinking it a good joke; so we went along with the prank since none of us had fallen into the sea.

It was a rough sea. We were rolled and tossed about with the spray in our faces until we reached the breakwater of logs. As we approached the dock there was much activity: longshoremen carrying freight here and there, Eskimos in their colorful parkas made of printed calico, and curious natives waiting to welcome us and the *North Star* to Nome. Perce was already on the dock. He had preceded us on the *North Star* launch.

Nome wasn't large. It sits out on a sand spit. The huge gold dredges owned by the mining and smelting company, the main industry, employed over one hundred and fifty men. On the main street, running parallel to the sea, were several old saloons; a couple of stores that carried hardware, clothing, food, and everything one would need to survive; boarding houses; old rundown buildings; cafes connected to the saloons where you could get a large slice of ham, and all the eggs and fried potatoes you could eat, with a pile of toast for two dollars and fifty cents.

There were two well constructed buildings on the main street, owned by the government and the bank. They had enormous septic tanks in the basements that drained off into the gravel near the sea. All the other toilets in Nome were chemical, and the cans were picked up once a week. We were told the garbage man had offered fifty thousand dollars to any man who would take over the business and marry his daughter. He had no takers.

Perce and I went up to the government school. We looked at parkas and ivory articles made by the Eskimos of King Island. The ivory was etched with walrus, seals, fox, bear and other designs. In the summer the King Island Eskimos camp out in tents on the outskirts of Nome to sell their wares. We needed parkas, but they were rather fancy and priced fifty dollars or more. We were short of cash and we figured if the Eskimos made their own parkas there would be someone in the village to make ours.

Walking around the town, Perce and I saw our first dog team, ten beautiful, matched white huskies, owned by one of the madams. The *North Star* launch was ready to leave the dock; so we and Stuart Widener jumped aboard. We had seen enough of Nome.

Stuart told us that Kathryn, his wife, had been seasick the entire trip and had spent most of her time in their stateroom. In fact, she had gone to bed the minute she boarded ship. Because of this, Stuart spent a great deal of time with us.

By this time the sea was really rough. We were tossed back and forth, up and down, with heavy waves going over the launch. Drenched to the skin, we reached the ship. No platform this time! We climbed the ladder on the side of the ship. It seemed safer.

The *North Star* blasted her whistle. The two launches came alongside. The other passengers were aboard. We were on our way to Galovin, where we said goodbye to

Mrs. Benawa. Our last night aboard was warm. The sun had just set and would soon be up again. The sky had a reddish tinge. The sea had calmed and we were sailing along as on a cloud. Stuart, Hemsing, Perce and I went topside. Hemsing and family were going to Kotzebue, where he was to be the reindeer boss. Perce was to care for the reindeer herd around Norton Sound near our station. We knew very little about reindeer; so we were comparing notes. We would be leaving our new friends and comrades the next day.

At Saint Michael, we left the *North Star*. We had a wonderful trip; now it was time to say goodbye. I gave the captain a big hug and kiss much to the surprise of everyone, especially the captain. Clarise hated to see us leave. As we stood on the platform being lowered to the lighter, the crew and passengers were leaning over the rail smiling and waving.

Herb Johnson had brought the lighter and barge out to the ship for us and our supplies. Herb ran the trading post for Frank Williams, who had the mail run to Kotzebue. We were to stay with the Johnsons while in Saint Michael. We carried our grips up to the house where we met Mrs. Johnson and the teachers from Stebbins. They seemed very young. Mrs. Johnson looked as if the Alaskan weather had taken its toll, but I really liked her. She seemed straightforward and would be a true friend. You had to be a bit hardboiled to live in the North. Even the Rhode Island Red chickens that the Johnsons kept grew feathers on their legs. Everyone and everything had to adapt.

Saint Michael had been a fort in the Yukon Gold Rush days of '98 before the railroad was built from Seward to Fairbanks. There were old barracks buildings. The Johnsons lived in the officers' quarters, not a bad house, but it had high ceilings. The Eskimos had built their homes of lumber salvaged from abandoned buildings. Saint Michael looked like a set for a western movie.

On the waterfront the Northern Commercial Company had a warehouse and trading post. Perce bought some fawn skins for a parka and winter mukluks. I wanted to buy mine in Chaneliak from the Eskimos. If the Eskimo women could keep warm I could wear the same kind of parka they wore.

Along the shore and slews dozens of old stern wheelers were beached. We tramped through several that were still not too destroyed. They were enormous grand old boats with gold leaf ornamented bars, fancy door knobs and hinges of brass or copper. They had cost thousands of dollars to build. It is said they paid for themselves in one trip up the Yukon to the gold fields. Perce took a fire extinguisher and later made ash trays and a fruit dish from the copper in it.

Still standing was an old Russian church left from the days when Russia owned Alaska. Inside was a raised life-sized picture of Christ's body lying on the altar with many jewels around it. The stations of the cross were represented by jeweled pictures. Sailors from the Coast Guard boat came while we were there and took some gems and pictures out of the church. Herb wired the ship; the ship returned and the property was returned.

After two days with the Johnsons, we left Saint Michael. Otto Pollie loaded our supplies on his twenty-four foot boat for the last leg of our journey through the back canals. Many ducks and geese were in the water. It was misty and a little cold. The coloring of the sky with its reds and blues was spectacular. We passed by a reindeer camp but did not see any reindeer.

We found out most small boats in Alaska had no privacy and no toilets. One just carried a large coffee can and went to the stern of the boat.

We crossed the open water of Norton Sound and the calm seas of Pastol Bay. Point Romanof stood on the only little hill in hundreds of miles of flat tundra. Anchoring off the north mouth of the Yukon, we had a dinner of canned reindeer meat and spent the night.

The next morning at 2:00 a.m., I climbed out of the hold of the boat, where I had slept on top of our grocery supplies for the coming year. Looking across the flattest, quietest grass-covered country I had ever seen, I observed many varieties of water birds flying here and there, darting into the water and coming up with fish in their bills. Broods of ducklings glided along the brown surface of the water. The loud honking of geese sounded in the distance. To the right stood a tall, wireless pole and two cabins that were tilted to one side and sank in the middle. Near the edge of the water was a figure watching us. I waved, and he answered with an enormous grin on his face. I could now see the large black and white sign on one of the cabins, which read in bold print, "Northern Commercial Company, Kotlik, Alaska."

In a few minutes we turned into a narrow slew. There was our new home, Chaneliak, an Eskimo village. It was 4:00 a.m. as we docked in front of the school building constructed from an old barrack from Saint Michael. The largest structure in the village, it had our living quarters in the rear. As we were getting off the boat, an Eskimo boy ran out of one of the cabins, jumped into a dory and came across the slew to us with a wide smile. Extending his hand, he said *Waka,* turned around and began to carry the largest boxes into the building. One box with honey had been damaged; the honey was oozing out. When the boy picked up the box, he began to lick his fingers, then to my amazement wiped the entire box and licked his hands like a cub bear. Apparently it was the first time he had tasted honey.

The only other figure among the closely built log cabins across the slew was a lone Eskimo woman dressed in a dingy yellow print cloth parka. Her bent body gave the impression of great weariness. She was waving her hand in front of her face trying to keep the millions of mosquitoes from feasting on her. I thought it strange that only this solitary woman and a boy were in the village. Otto told me the people were camped not far away along the river and the sea, salmon fishing and drying the fish for their winter supply. Each family needed several hundred dried fish for themselves and their dogs, since each dog ate a fish a day. He said the families would return in September before the Yukon froze.

The sun was now high in the sky; the mosquitoes were eating us alive. All our supplies were in the schoolhouse, thanks to our volunteer, Joe Aparezuk. This building, like the one I had seen at the mouth of the Yukon, was sunken in the middle and reminded me of a boat. As you walked in there was an entrance hall about eight feet square, then a large classroom twenty-five by forty. On the north side of the room was a row of double windows locked tight and never opened, secured so that no air or snow could get through. Above one window a small opening ten inches square was cut through the wall. A plug connected to a long wooden handle could be slid aside to let in a little fresh air. In one corner was the stove, a fifty gallon gasoline barrel, that burned wood or that terrible Alaskan coal. I thought about our experience at Petersburg. We would do something about that. In neat rows were twenty-five pupils' desks and a teacher's desk.

At the back of the classroom a door led into a storeroom where a ladder ascended to yet another storage area. From the storeroom we entered a small living room adequately furnished. To the left was a kitchen with a coal burning stove. Near the stove was a fifty-gallon barrel where ice was melted for water in the winter. In summer, the barrels would be put outside at the corners of the building to catch the rain. These were the two sources of our water supply. There was no running water on the tundra.

A bedroom opened off the kitchen, and a back porch held a chemical toilet that had to be emptied on the tundra. (This was pioneering!)

At the back of the building a boardwalk led to the ice house. A shop, as large as the classroom, was to the south; and there was an outside toilet for the children. Now that we had inspected everything, we were exhausted, so to bed we went without more delay. Thus began five years of experiences, living and working in the Eskimo village of Chaneliak.

II. Frontier Living

We had several visitors our first evening. They came in their small dories with outboard motors. Everyone seemed pleased to have us. Some just sat for an hour or so, not saying a word and then quietly left. Others wanted pills and medicine for their sores and cuts. The visitors didn't expect us to carry on a conversation; but it was apparent that there was a great deal of medical work to be done and the Eskimos depended on us to do it.

The reason for this situation seemed to be that for eight years, Mrs. Pettrie, my predecessor, had been the only person to teach and care for the people of Chaneliak, Pastolik and Kotlik. She was not a teacher: she was an R.N., trained at the Indian Hospital in Tacoma, Washington. Previous to 1930, the year of her arrival, there had been no school, no teacher, no nurse.

Very few Eskimo women spoke English. The men, however, had knowledge of the language from contacts made while working on the river boats or selling their furs to traders.

For the next week, we cleaned, unpacked, checked medical and school supplies. To our dismay, we found that one-third of our year's groceries was missing. They had been put on the railroad and shipped to Fairbanks. We also readied the classroom. There were medical books and instructional manuals, but few library books for either children or adults.

Since freeze-up was getting closer, most of the families had returned. We opened school. Eighteen children arrived, ranging in age from six to sixteen, all smiling and happy. The girls wore dirty dresses and cloth parkas. The boys, in their overalls, were somewhat cleaner. Not until I learned more about the culture was there a clue to this surprising difference.

The fact was the men and boys used the *khasgii* or community house as a bath and sweat house. This structure was to be found in every Eskimo winter village in Alaska prior to the establishment of white settlements.

In Chaneliak, the *khasgii* (somtimes spelled *kashim*) was near the center of the village. It was much larger than the dwellings, about 25 feet by 30 feet and 15 feet high at the smoke hole. The walls were of split logs placed vertically with the plane facing inwards. The floor was of hewed planks. About three and one-half feet from the walls, small logs were placed around the edge of the room for sleeping places. There was, as well, a broad sleeping bench about three feet above the small logs. The roof was made of planks covered with a foot or more of tundra moss.

The *kasgii* served a variety of purposes. It was a workshop for repairing sleds, kayaks, and small gear; a place for men and boys to lounge, gossip and tell stories; and a hostelry for visiting men. At night, it would be a gathering place for people of all ages and both sexes, a setting for games or festivals, or a rehearsal hall for songs and dances. When we arrived, it was used only by men and boys for bathing and, occasionally, for sleeping.

The next day, the Eskimo called Waska came over about 6:30 a.m. saying I was needed in the village. I couldn't quite figure out what he wanted me to do, but Perce said, "I think his wife is having a baby and they expect you to deliver it." Was I surprised! How would I do this?

Gathering up some supplies, I went across the slew in a boat. After examining his wife, I asked Waska who had helped Mrs. Pettrie. "Monica," he replied. "Go get Monica," quoth I.

Monica didn't speak a word of English, but understood me. I told her to stay, that I would be back shortly. I didn't think the baby would come for an hour.

Dashing back to the school, I found a book Mrs. Pettrie had left which described exactly how to deliver a baby. I have never read and learned so much in an hour in my whole life. I had been in the delivery room once, when a close friend gave birth, but otherwise knew very little. After absorbing as much knowledge as possible, back I went to the cabin. Mrs. Waska was having her pains closer together. She was kneeling and bending over a box on a bed made of boards with reindeer skins thrown over them. All of a sudden, the baby's head appeared and out he popped on the reindeer skins.

When I picked him up he urinated in my face and everyone guffawed. I could hardly stop laughing, but took him by his heels and slapped his little buttocks. He yelled with a good set of lungs.

Monica wiped out his mouth; I waited for about ten minutes and then when the beat had stopped, I tied and cut the cord to the afterbirth, which was put in a bucket and taken out on the tundra and buried.

After dropping argyrol in the baby's eyes, I proceeded to oil him. What a mess! I thought I would never clean the reindeer hair off his little body. Finally, I dressed him and gave him warm water to drink.

All the village women were bringing clothes and flannels to wrap the baby. They had a cultural belief that it was bad luck and the baby would not survive if clothes were made before birth. This seemed very strange to me.

The infant was well; all the excitement was over. The rest of the family unrolled their skins on the floor and went back to bed; clothes, boots and all. The baby lay safe in his mother's arms and Waska was happy to have a new son, whom he called George.

The next morning there was another surprise. At eight o'clock, Waska brought the baby over for its first bath. This went on for seven days, which was the common practice. Much to my satisfaction, the child was healthy and the cord was almost dry.

Then Marion Prince came with an ear infection. I knew now we would be doctor and nurse as well as teacher and guardian for this village and the surrounding country. That meant we had better get medical advice. I wrote to Margaret Weightman at Petersburg and my old friend, Dr. Charles Falk, Sr, at Eureka. We had been informed that Alma Carlson, the field nurse, would not be able to come until the following fall or later. Luckily, Mrs. Pettrie had left many medical books. We had our work cut out for us.

The next day, with the temperature at 40 above zero, Herb Johnson arrived with coal and provisions on the barge for Frank Williams' trading post in the village. He had breakfast and dinner with us, stayed the night, and started back to Saint Michael at daylight.

Any non-Eskimos traveling through town lodged at the school. There was no place else to stay. Besides, that was the only way to get news. We enjoyed the visitors.

Every day, the weather seemed to be colder. I taught in the morning. There were still several children at the camps. Alex Okitkum, the trader for Frank Williams at Chaneliak, asked us to go on his boat, the *Daisy*, to Pastolik.

Alex had a 30 foot-craft with an inboard motor and a cabin, the only boat of that size at Chaneliak. On the way, Alex stopped and pulled up his tom cod trap, filled with squirming fish. A tom cod trap is made of strips of driftwood and is about four or five feet across and eight to ten feet long. Large poles are attached to the trap and pounded into the mud at the bottom of the slew. The fish swim into the funnel at the top of the trap and can't get out.

The trap held more than eight hundred fish, a good catch for one day.

Near Pastolik, we saw an old dredge. It had been used to open the north mouth of the Yukon in the Gold Rush days of 1898; in 1937, it was filling up again. Only small boats could enter. It was unlikely it would ever be reopened since Alaska now had the railroad to Nenana, where it met its own cargo vessels, which plied the Tanana and Yukon Rivers. We didn't go into the village at Pastolik as the Eskimos had not returned from camp.

On the way back Alex stopped to see his brother Tom at the fish camp on the tundra. The tundra is important to the Eskimo. It has a cover of sphagnum that forms a protective coat from the heat of the sun and keeps the ice from melting farther than a few inches below the surface. It is covered with moss berries, tall grass, low cranberries and willows. There were ten tents at the camp and hundreds of salmon drying on the pole racks. The women and girls were cleaning the fish and cutting off the heads, which they boiled and ate or fed to the dogs. They then split the fish, removing the back bone but leaving the tail, and hung them over the racks to dry. I saw one of the older girls and asked her to come to school. An old lady wanted to give me some low bush cranberries that grow on the tundra, are gathered in the fall, and are kept for the winter. The cranberries are small and sour. The children had already given me too many; so I declined.

Father Lonneux arrived on Sunday from Stebbins Village. We went to church in the evening to introduce ourselves. While Father played the phonograph for the Eskimos, we listened. Everyone from the village was there. After prayers, when the Eskimos went home, we stayed a little longer. Father, who seemed interested in the people, offered to help us get settled and become acquainted with the customs and the country.

He told us he was born in Belgium and educated in Europe in the Jesuit order. His people had owned textile mills in Belgium since the first world war. From them he received twenty-five hundred dollars a year to help the Eskimos. "I stay here six months," he said, "then return to Stebbins for six months."

I asked him to dinner, an invitation he seemed happy to accept. Perce had been hunting ducks and geese every day. They would soon be gone on their flight south. We were enjoying the luxury while we could. We would have both ducks and a goose for dinner.

Joe Usiak, the trader for the Northern Commercial Company, who lived at the mouth of the slew, came to inform us that the remainder of our groceries had arrived on the *Masabe* from upriver and would be unloaded in the morning. With him was a young boy from Eklutna, the Indian Industrial School near Anchorage. The boy had a job as deck hand on the *Masabe.* Traveling up and down the Yukon, he met many people and enjoyed his work. They visited for an hour. The next morning Father took Perce in his outboard motor boat to get the groceries. We received everything but one box of hams and other canned meats. Someone wanted that box of meats more than we did. I was glad to have the supplies but frustrated because we had no place to put everything.

Preparing for the mail run was a periodic project. There was a great deal of paperwork for both of us to do. Then as now, the government needed four copies of everything. There were various forms to fill out and inventories to take. Father helped me with Joe Aparezuk's orphan's report. We were trying to get funds to assist his grandmother with his support. At last the mail was ready including packages containing baskets made of coiled tundra grass, which I was sending to my folks and a friend. Alex would take the lot to Saint Michael, where it would be loaded on the *Baranoff* bound for Seattle.

It was the end of September and the birds had not flown south yet. The rain, coming down in bucketfuls, filled our water barrels at the corners of the building. The wind howled from the east at fifty miles an hour. Alex returned with a raft of logs from Saint Michael for the village and the school. Some of the logs would be used for cabins and others for firewood. The Eskimos had small cookstoves in their cabins, their only source of heat.

On the last day of September, twenty-five children were in school. I was teaching them to read, to write letters, know their numbers, and to do practical things like knitting and baking yeast bread. Their educational needs were simple; most of these people would travel only a few miles from their village.

At 3:15 p.m. Cyril Okitkun, Alex's brother, came running through the doorway. "Come quick! Alex's wife Ann is having a baby," he called out. I snatched some things I would need, but when we burst into the home, Baby Girl had already arrived. Hers was a premature birth of eight months. Alex found a box and we filled hot water bottles to make an incubator. After an hour I went back to school for more supplies. Just as I arrived at school, Cyril came running after me. Another baby had come. We rushed back. This baby was not breathing. I lifted the little boy by his feet and slapped him hard on the buttocks. The thin pitiful little creature, weighing about two pounds, started to breathe, but I was afraid not for long. At 5:30 p.m., I went home; he died at six. The twin girl might live, but she was a blue baby and very tiny too.

This wasn't an easy time for me. My first delivery had

been a normal birth, but I was out of my depth now. I knew so little, and there was no help nearer than Mountain Village, two hundred miles farther up the Yukon.

In early October, the girls were knitting gloves, mittens, sweaters and spiral socks. I had brought yarn. Father had many skeins at the church and didn't know what to do with them, so had been happy to give them to me for the girls. In the rain I went to the village to give Alex's and Ann's baby her feeding of kilm, and to change and bathe her. Her stool was black and dark brown. I gave her an enema. She was so small and cute; she even smiled at me. She was like a little brown doll weighing about two and one half pounds. I was wishing she would live but knew she would never be strong. For eight days I took care of her but on the ninth day she died. Perce helped Alex make the second coffin. On a frosty, sunny morning she was buried next to her brother on top of the tundra, a mile from the village.

The Northern Commercial man came with our freight bill. Never before was I so angry. It cost fifty dollars to ship 2,300 pounds to Saint Michael by boat but $109.34 to send 1,600 pounds by Alaskan Railroad. There is always a first and last time for everything: no more railroad freight for me!

Mary Ann came from Pastolik with Perce's parka made from the fawn skins he had bought at Saint Michael. She had done a beautiful job and it fit perfectly. To measure Perce she had just looked at him and turned him around several times. She sized our mukluks by looking at our feet. She was also making me an Arctic hare parka. The fur was worn next to one's clothing and a canvas or cloth parka was worn over it. I had bought a wolverine ruff from Bush on the *North Star*. Mary Ann would use it on the hood.

Everything outside was frosty. It looked like fairyland. While the girls knitted, I was making a heavy maroon sweater for Perce. He had been helping the men and boys in the shop to fashion steel knives from files and to make handles for them from reindeer antlers. He had also been putting shiplap and insulation on the outside of the school building. Roy Hunt was building a log cabin; Alex and Charlie Prince were each adding another room to theirs.

Perce was helping every day that weather permitted.

When it was cold and windy, Perce worked in the shop with the school boys and the men, making library tables, shelves, chairs and kayaks. They made kites too. One day when it was sunny and windy, out on the tundra went the entire village to fly kites. They had a great time. This was a new experience for everyone. October 18, Alaska Day, was a holiday. There was a skiff of snow. Chaneliak slew was freezing over in places, barring kayaks; so all the men able to hunt carried their kayaks to the open water on the Yukon, then paddled to the sea on Norton Sound to hunt seal. It was a busy time, making new kayaks and sleds and mending old ones.

Leo Aparezuk, with his wife Lea's help, was building a new kayak. The frame was made of spruce wood strips, which were softened in hot water so that they could be bent to the needed shape. In previous times, kayaks were covered with seal skins, but Leo was using heavy canvas bought from the trader. The kayak was eighteen feet long and two feet wide amidships. The top was covered except for an open cockpit at the center, large enough for a man to sit in. There was a coaming about the cockpit around which the gut parka of the occupant could be tied tight, making the kayak unsinkable. Kayak and man could capsize and recover with little danger. This type of canoe was universal among the Alaskan Eskimos. It was used among the ice floes to hunt walrus; but in our village it had great value in penetrating the slews, lakes, and lagoons to hunt muskrat, fox, mink, water fowl, and seal. It also bore the men into reindeer and beaver country.

It was clean-up week. The boys were taking care of the wood pile. The girls were in the classroom arranging the books and magazines on the new shelves in the corner we had made into a library. The library was not only for the school children, but for adults too. Father joined in the project and brought over some books and magazines. However, he cut out from the magazines the pictures he didn't want the natives to see. Rather strange, I thought.

We had a pet weasel in the woodpile. He had changed to his winter coat, a beautiful soft white. When we called, he would poke his head out of his hiding place as if to say,

"Hello, I'm here. Have you something for me to eat?"

Perce put a window in Roy Hunt's new cabin and helped Alex put the *Daisy* in dry dock for the winter. The children made sketches of the boat and the village. They were clever with their hands, doing excellent drawings. It was a real pleasure to teach in Chaneliak. Everyone was so good. There were no discipline problems with the children or adults; they were all happy and smiling.

Interestingly, the small children were babied. Even a five-year-old might have a nursing bottle of canned milk, or a three-year-old might be sucking from his mother's breast. The Eskimos seemed never to correct their children.

Roy's cabin was almost finished. Perce had cut the battens to use in chinking, when another baby girl was born at Roy's house. I was called at 8:20 p.m. Monica wasn't well so I was alone: I really needed her help, but thank goodness, the baby was healthy and strong. These little babies have to be tough to survive.

Mail arrived. It came once a month if we were lucky and someone brought it from Saint Michael. It required two hours to read because there were so many reports and orders from the Juneau office; answering took much longer.

Joe Uisuk came by and wanted us to ride in the dory with the outboard motor to hunt seal in Norton Sound. We refused, because the men in the village were unhappy with Joe for using his outboard when hunting seal among their kayaks. I asked him to use his kayak. He was a cripple: one leg was shorter than the other: so it was easier to use the dory with the outboard motor. However, he said he would stop using the dory.

In late October the water was freezing and there was a little rain. We decorated for Halloween and made paper bag masks. The children, creative and humorous, produced some very funny masks. There was great anticipation as they had never had a Halloween party. At noon on Halloween, the parents arrived. Everyone joined in the fun: drop the handkerchief, pin the tail on the donkey, blind man's buff—no matter what the game, everyone played and laughed. I served cookies the girls had made, raisins, and cocoa for refreshments. At three o'clock the party was over. Each child and adult thanked me and shook hands. The Eskimos love to shake hands when they meet and when they say good-bye.

The freeze-up arrived. The children and women fished through the ice for cod with hooks at the end of willow sticks. They skated on the ponds near the village. While they skated and fished I did office work and wrote to the Red Cross for Christmas boxes for the children. Perce painted the inside of the water barrels and brought them into the kitchen to melt ice for water in the winter.

On the radio we heard our friends from the *North Star,* Kathryn and Stuart Widener, telling the Nome teachers that many bears and wolves had been sighted in the Kotzebue country. Perce wished he could be there for the big game hunting. He did take time off to hunt rabbit and ptarmigan. Ptarmigans are a kind of grouse that have feathered feet and change from white in winter to a speckled brown in summer. They reminded me of mountain quail and are very good eating. When the first light snow fell, Perce went to the village and divided among the men the lumber Herb Johnson had brought from Saint Michael.

By November, it was snowing heavily and the ice was getting thicker. I saw a dog team in the distance. It had come from Hamilton and was on its way to Saint Michael to collect the mail.

The school girls made cloth bunnies stuffed with reindeer hair, wrote letters to a school in Arcata, California, and made drawings of the village and of the animals around Chaneliak. We sent these things to the Red Cross in exchange for Christmas packages. They also knit gloves, mittens, sweaters, and spiral socks for Christmas gifts to family members. Perce made handles for their knitting bags. The girls were happy with their handwork. These were all new experiences for them; they had learned many useful things in the three months we had been in Chaneliak, and we were learning also.

Mary Ann brought my Arctic hare parka. Oliva Mike made my winter mukluks but she needed hard seal soles; so I got the soles from Titina Hunt. The tops were made of reindeer skins with the hair outside and sported a double top border of felt with braided yarn drawn through and tasseled at the end. The yarn tied tightly around the legs to keep out the snow and cold. If you put tundra grass in the bottom and wore heavy socks, your feet were toasty warm. Perce was helping Cyril and his brother Tom build new sleds. The Government provided the hickory wood and steel runners. A sled could be built with one piece of hickory 12'x1'x2" thick. Most sleds were twelve feet long. Tom was also making a bed. The Eskimos made their beds of the lumber they had received from Saint Michael. A six inch board was nailed around the edge of a solid frame. Reindeer hides were thrown on the frame. Four legs were usually added.

The southwest wind was blowing a gale. It was thirty-six above; the ice was melting fast. Hooper Bay and Nome were flooding. The ice in the slew and the Yukon had gone out. There was no school because of high tide. The houses in the village had a few inches of water around them: three feet more and we would have had water in the school room. Alex brought a dory over for us. Cyril went to Pastolik for a gas boat to take Father and Perce to Hamilton for supplies and mail. They got up the Yukon a few miles, the boat iced up and they returned. Fortunately the weather turned colder, the tide went down and we were safe.

During the time of high water, the older girls were walking over the tundra to the Northern Commerical store at the mouth of the slew. I had to scold them. It was just someplace to go, but it was dangerous because the ice had melted and one could step into a hole several feet deep and would be unable to get out without help. They could have broken an ankle or a leg; besides they were needed at home. Father and we seemed to be the authority figures for all the Eskimos within a radius of a hundred miles or more. They followed our orders without question.

Perce worked every day and early evenings with the men and boys in the shop. The boys were making wooden toys for all the children under eighteen in the village. The three older boys, Tom Prince, Joe Aparezuk, and David Joe, were making their first sled. The boys remained in school until they had made a sled and trained five dogs to pull it, so that they could make a living hunting fur animals. Then their formal education would end.

Since the high tide, the Yukon wasn't frozen hard enough to get ice, so Perce and I filled the barrels in the kitchen with snow. It took tons to get enough water to drink and cook; washing clothes or taking a bath was a luxury.

All the girls were making rag dolls for Christmas. Some of the older girls were making dresses for themselves, as the school had the only sewing machine in the village. They used no patterns, and all their dresses fit like a sack tied in the middle. They were lucky if the dress was clean. Some had one dress, others two.

The north wind had been blowing for a week and it was almost Thanksgiving; so freeze-up was certain this time. I had been cleaning and putting up new curtains. We began to practice our songs for Christmas. In some, the men and women joined the children in two-part singing. Our library was a great success during this cold season. People from our village and from Kotlik and Pastolik came at different times, sometimes during school. They, as well as the children, were learning to read and write. We had bought walrus tusks in Nome at seventy-five cents a pound for the Eskimos to carve. Perce carved ivory buttons for the girls' dresses. Waska, one of the men, made a cribbage board, others carved small animals like fox, bear, and seals.

It was eighteen above on Thanksgiving. Father came to dinner. We had canned chicken with dumplings, canned carrots, canned creamed potatoes, pineapple salad, muffins, and mince pie, plus all the trimmings: olives, pickles, honey, and jelly. The table was decorated with brown and orange willow brush. We all ate too much and I thought I had better be careful or I would be as big as a mountain. However, with Perce teasing if I gained and complaining if I didn't eat, it was a bit difficult to diet.

Alex and Roy were hauling blocks of ice for us from the Yukon. I hadn't done laundry for a month because of lack of water. Now I could.

At the end of November, the temperature was six above. The sun was shining when I took my first dog sled ride. Cyril took me to Kotlik, six miles from Chaneliak. He had put reindeer skins on the bottom of the sled, I threw a sleeping bag on top and covered up with two blankets. We bumped along in the slew until we reached the main Yukon, then sailed along on the ice. Another team going to Hamilton came alongside us. The musher visited with Cyril about acquaintances and the condition of the ice on the way to Saint Michael; then he sped on his way. He was faster: he had ten dogs and we had five. It was hard riding. I decided next time I would bring a pillow. When the dogs stopped, which they did, to do their toilet, the jolt was like hitting another car in an accident. There were no reins; so to start the dogs you let go the brake and yelled, "Mush!" After the dogs were running, if you wanted them to turn right you shouted, "Gee," or to the left "Haw!" To stop you stepped on the brake and shouted "Whoa." Riding in a sled on the Yukon was like being on a race track. The bank is higher than the river, and when the dogs see another team, they race along to catch up. If there is a mean dog in either team, the musher has his hands full to keep them from fighting. Malamutes like to fight.

Joe Uisuk came along with his team and some loose dogs. Cyril had all he could do to keep the animals apart by grabbing his lead dog until Joe's team had passed.

A little before eleven we reached Kotlik. It was a larger village than I expected. The houses were empty except the two Andrews family homes. We went to their houses to visit and to tell them we were at Chaneliak to help them with medicines or to be of service in any other way we could. Their houses had four rooms and were very clean. I was pleasantly surprised, since the Cheneliak houses were only one or two rooms and not too clean. I was thinking the Chaneliak Eskimos should take lessons from the Andrews in keeping their places cleaner.

Kotlik people even had large ranges for cooking while the ones at Cheneliak were small cast iron stoves. The floors were covered with linoleum, the walls with flowered wallpaper. Covered fifty gallon water tanks like ours were in the kitchen for melting ice. The entrance hall was clean. They didn't have frozen fish or seal meat stored in the entrance and smelling to high heaven. The caches for fish and other food were built outside the houses. The yards were clean and there were plank walkways through the entire village.

Each dog had its own little house made of logs or of a fifty gallon barrel half buried in the tundra or covered with sod for warmth. Wood was cut and split, some of it stacked in the shed.

In the center of the village was a small Russian church that looked ready to fall down. It wasn't interesting like the Russian church at Saint Michael because all the artifacts had been removed. It was empty. The natives did not use it, as they were Roman Catholic and came to Cheneliak for Mass. At the back of the church was a graveyard.

After looking at some fawn skin parkas the Andrews had for sale, we ended our visit. These people seemed more familiar with the white man's ways and the English language than our villagers.

When we left, the sun was shining and I just sat looking at the clear blue sky. Point Romanof was off in the distance covered with a blanket of snow. It looked like a big mud pie thrown down and stepped on, then covered with white frosting.

It was a typical Sunday. Alex Johnson, the mailman, came with his team of twenty-four dogs, quite a sight. He wore a parka of Unalakeet squirrel. It was a very pretty fur, orange and grey with brown spots. All the Eskimos from Kotlik and Pastolik were in the village for church.

Mary Ann came to school to deliver my parka and boots. I paid her eight dollars and one hundred pounds of flour.

Many visitors came to see and use the library and to get medicine, especially cod liver oil, which we gave out by the gallons.

There was little daylight now in Chaneliak. Darkness fell at 2:30 p.m. and lasted until 9:00 a.m.

On the radio we heard Point Barrow. The mail team had disappeared near Wainright. When the bodies were found, they had been chewed by wolves. This country is cruel and cold.

We were invited to the church to see an Eskimo show. Father had a great many masks made by Eskimos. In the Arctic North the masks were delicately crafted. They were carved and painted wood face pieces. Feathers and small carvings representing animals and fish were attached to them. Red, black, and blue were the predominant colors. Animal fat was mixed with charcoal and berry juices to make pigments. Sometimes large areas were left unpainted as were most of the masks Father had in his collection. Several of the masks were half-man-half-animal or fish. Before the white man came to Alaska the shamans had worn the masks and danced as part of ceremonies to bring success in fishing and hunting.

When the show began, three drummers were sitting cross-legged on the floor singing a song and accompanying the movements of the dancers with staccato beats on large tambourine-like drums. These were about three feet across with an eight inch handle resembling a broomstick. The song told the story of the dancers' adventures. The dancers performed jerky motions with arms, head, trunk, and legs, stamping one foot to the rhythm of the beat.

Next came four gamblers wearing wooden masks. They threw down the cards, shouting at one another. They jumped up and down, hit one another in mock battle, and rolled on the floor saying everyone was cheating. Then one man, dressed as a dog, rushed in and chased them all home. The skit was very funny; everyone was laughing and having a good time.

Waska, or Ptarmigan as he was called, was half Russian. He entertained us with a Russian dance to music from the phonograph.

Last, in jumped a player costumed as a gorilla, frightening the children and doing all the things monkeys do. He tried to get Perce and me to act with him. We declined. The audience, especially the children, were screaming with laughter. Thus ended the show.

Behind the masks, everyone had taken on a different character. The evening was a great success.

December arrived. Everyone was looking forward to Christmas. The women came to school to sing Christmas carols for the program we were planning. They sang "Silent Night" and "Oh, Come All Ye Faithful" in Eskimo. The men came in the evening. The part singing in English, especially for the women who had little exposure to the language, took a great deal of practice. Most of them came to school every day and tried hard to learn the songs. After practicing at school with no accompaniment, we would go to the church and do it all again with the little organ.

For three weeks the weather was terrible; the northeast wind blew the stovepipe off the school building again and again. The snow was swirling in every direction; you couldn't see five feet in front of you. The door flew open and the front entrance was full of snow. Wind blowing through the keyhole into the classroom built a tall slender pile of snow from the floor to the keyhole. The foot-square shutter cut through the wall above the window had to be closed tight. We once left the shutter in our bedroom open during a storm and awoke to a pile of snow on our bed. The shutters supplied the only fresh air in the rooms.

Before the storm, ten men from the village had gone hunting reindeer. They had brought back enough meat for everyone in the village. We received two carcasses, which we hung in the ice shed. Everyone was delighted to have the taste of fresh meat.

Perce and the boys were finishing and painting the toys. The smaller boys had made ducks and animals with wheels; the older boys had fashioned boats and kayaks. Tom Prince constructed a toy that went around like a merry-go-round for his younger brother. For all the little girls, the school girls had made rag dolls stuffed with reindeer hair. Every child, even the babies, had a handmade toy. I photographed the school children with the toys they had made. The film was sent to a friend in California to be developed. Later the children would be surprised with a photo of themselves.

Each day we had more patients to treat. Perce took care of the men and I helped the women and children. Many had syphilitic eye and ear infections. I learned that the women chewed food before putting it into the mouths of their babies. When the women came to school to practice, Mamie, one of my best students, acted as interpreter. With her help, I explained to them they were infecting their children with the disease.

In addition, I engaged the help of the Father in this

matter. Apparently, the people understood and stopped the practice.

It was the fifteenth of December, only ten more days to Christmas. Father gave me some long wool coats; these were set aside so the girls could make jackets for all the children next Christmas.

He also provided card games, word games, jigsaw puzzles, soap, toothbrushes and socks to put in the children's packages. We had finished wrapping the wooden toys. Everything was getting done a little at a time except the singing, which seemed to be getting worse instead of better.

Father had asked me to come to the church and help outfit everyone from head to toe. Everything was spread out on the tables and benches; caps, mittens, scarfs, bolts of material, sweaters, underwear, even some fancy combs for women's hair.

Pine trees were many miles up the Yukon; so Starkey brought us a willow and some branches. The willow made a very strange-looking Christmas tree. Perce nailed more branches on it, with which it was odder than ever, but it smelled like the outdoors. When the children decorated it with paper chains, cut-out snow flakes, small wooden reindeer and strings of popcorn, it looked something like a Christmas tree.

Perce made a huge screen corn popper. First, we tried to use it with the stove's front door open. We smoked ourselves out of the classroom. Then we built a big fire in the barrel stove and popped the corn on top. That worked better. The older girls looked in my cookbook for a recipe for popcorn balls. What a mess they made in my kitchen! But what fun they had, with their sticky hands and dresses!

Two days before Christmas Eve, ours was a busy place. The oldest girls, Margaret and Agnes, were making cookies and roasting peanuts while the others filled Christmas sacks with nuts, raisins, candy, and popcorn balls. Some of the children were making their costumes.

Roy Hunt, our comic, was fashioning a reindeer costume for his act in a play at the church on Christmas night. He and Perce went out for some old reindeer horns that Perce had seen about eight miles from the village.

When Christmas Eve arrived, the temperature was 16 degrees above zero and the sky was very dark. We had taken all the desks out of the classroom to provide seating space for the audience. At 5:30, I rang the bell for the children to come and be dressed for their parts. All arrived wearing their new clothes and saying, "Merry Christmas."

Every child shook hands with Perce and me. At 6:00, the bell rang for the audience. We went through the same ritual of Christmas greetings and hand shakes. The Eskimos liked shaking hands, not rubbing noses, thank goodness. We all have strange customs.

Everyone sat on the floor. It was a colorful and happy group, with the women and babies in matching bright calico parkas.

My little boys came to the front of the room singing "Jolly Old Saint Nick." They were having a difficult time with the words and were all singing in different keys. Each child was carrying a letter to spell out "Merry Christmas." The audience was laughing and enjoying every minute of it. Next came the chorus carrying lighted candles. Mary, Joseph and baby Jesus entered with the shepherds and the three kings. The Christmas story was narrated by Tom Prince, the oldest boy.

The chorus sang in two-part harmony "Silent Night" and "We Three Kings." "Oh, Come All Ye Faithful," in Eskimo, ended the program with the audience joining in the chorus.

Aparezuk, our Santa, arrived making fun of everyone. Two of the girls, wearing long stocking caps, were dressed as Santa's helpers. They danced around, giving out the packages and sacks of goodies. By then it was 11:00.

Everyone adjourned to the church for midnight Mass. With the wind howling and snowflakes falling, Father said Mass in Latin and led the songs in Eskimo. We were surely in a foreign country, a long way from California, but it was pleasant to be included in the festivities of the village. The evening ended with more "Merry Christmases" and handshakes, whereupon we returned to our living quarters.

Even on Christmas, we had clinic. Father was having his Santa at 2:00 p.m., When the bell rang, we dashed to the church, the last to arrive, as usual.

The benches had been placed around the edge of the room and in front of the altar. We had special front seats. The first performer to appear was Roy riding the reindeer. He had made a frame with space in the middle for a man's legs. The deer head moved up and down when pulled by the bridle. The frame was covered with real reindeer skins and had a tail sticking up in the air. Dummy deer legs were fastened to the side. Roy talked to the animal. Then he and the deer lay down only to jump up as a policeman dashed in.

The deer butted people in the audience to the accompaniment of screams of laughter. After being butted around the room, the policeman finally got hold of the bridle. At that moment, a big brown grizzly bear appeared and ran both the deer and the policeman out of the room. The bear was very grateful to take off that heavy bear head and suit.

Next came Santa. His attendants, dressed in old Moose Lodge uniforms, pulled a sled with a large cardboard box on it. Santa told Perce to open the box. Out leaped a little old man with whiskers. He handed us each a parcel, saying "Merry Christmas." Jumping off the sled, he took out a huge cigar and had a smoke. The deer, Santa, and all the attendants sat in the middle of the floor and gave out parcels. Santa threw confetti in the face of the people as they came to get their packages. They didn't like that.

Father would close the Christmas weekend with another show the next day. The people were to return to their villages on Monday.

The day after Christmas, with the temperature at four above, the people were coming to be doctored. A little after ten, one of the women came and told me Mary Andrews had given birth to a baby boy. I was surprised that I hadn't been called, but the Andrews were from Kotlik.

Quickly, I snatched my supplies and rushed to Chiklik's house where Mary was staying. Only the baby's face had been washed; he had not been bathed or oiled. After putting a piece of cotton on the cord, I proceeded to wash and oil him. He seemed to be well and strong, but Mary was still passing blood. I bathed her and didn't think about her condition until later.

Father was having his last entertainment before his return to Stebbins, the village where he would remain for six months. The show was to be at 6:00 and we didn't want to miss it. When we opened the door of the church, we saw a dummy lying on the floor. Soon, the medicine man arrived carrying a thick branch and a rope. He beat the dummy with his stick and tied the rope around its neck, raising its square head with big round red eyes and two sharp-pointed upright ears. The dummy looked as if it were asking for help. The medicine man jerked its head back and forth and dragged the dummy out of the room.

Next came Roy wearing a black mask. He had on dirty old clothes and carried a barrel covered over with a cloth, to represent a sourdough barrel. (The Eskimos make an alcoholic drink from sourdough).

He was drunk and fell over the barrel. Every few minutes he would put his little cup into the barrel and have a drink. He staggered around, had the heaves and passed out. In came three singers, one drummer and two dancers. The dancers carried eight-inch wooden hoops with feathers fastened around the edge.

One dancer knelt, the other stood. The singers began to chant in Eskimo. Very slowly, the dancers moved the tops of their bodies back and forth. The drummer called out the dance they were to do, such as imitating a fox or a bear. The singers sang louder; the drummer drummed faster; the dancers waved their hoops and swayed their bodies more and more rapidly until they were exhausted. Other dancers entered and took up the rhythm.

Returning, the drunk tried to imitate the dancers, bending, weaving, and falling down and rolling on the floor. In the next act, two visitors came to Chaneliak. The medicine man greeted them carrying a seal skin filled with trinkets and tricks. He traded with them until he had all their money.

In the last act, the white men were included. In came a real dory on wheels, holding two Eskimo cooks with a large kettle and pushed by four crew men, their faces painted white.

Everything went into the kettle: a cloth dog, a real

rabbit and fish, pepper, rubber wieners. After much stirring, the cooks tried to put the rabbit, fish and rubber wieners into the mouths of the crew. This made the crew unhappy. They began to hit the cooks with the food and to yell what bad cooks they were. Finally, they pushed boat and cooks out of the room.

There was also a take-off on me as a nurse. Roy, the nurse, was having a dreadful time trying to understand Eskimo. He had a big sealskin bag filled with forceps, pills, scissors, and many bottles of medicine. He came to me and said, "You sick." I decided I had better play the game.

"Yes," I replied, "I'm sick."

"What's the matter with you?" Roy asked.

"My belly and my head is sick." I said.

"You not sick," Roy declared.

"Yes, I am very sick." I began to hold my stomach and groan.

"No, you fool, you fool me, you not sick. You sit down; no medicine for you," insisted Roy.

Two people came in with faces swollen from toothache. "Open your mouth," ordered Roy. With a stick holding a large red swab, Roy swished around in their mouths. The patients pretended to gag. A three-foot tall old man with whiskers, wearing a dunce cap and dressed in dirty clothes, wanted pills to grow taller.

"Talk English," said Roy; but the ancient just jabbered Eskimo louder. The scene ended with Roy saying, "Funny people." The skits were amusing and very well done. I think I had surprised Roy by cooperating.

Father was very clever with his entertainments, using ridicule and satire, such as the sourdough and medicine man skits, to show the natives these things were no-noes. We invited Father to a post-Christmas dinner of reindeer roast with all the trimmings. The next day, he left for Stebbins.

I was bathing Mary's baby daily. He seemed fine, but Mary was running a temperature. Concluding that afterbirth must be left, I gave her penicillan and tried to force out more pieces of afterbirth. I succeeded. It smelled terrible. The next day her fever was gone and she was much better. She returned with her family to Kotlik.

On the last day of 1937, it was 15 below, with the north wind blowing a gale. On January 1 the temperature fell to twenty below, and that is mighty cold on the tundra. Your face will freeze in a few minutes if you don't rub it constantly and keep it covered. When the wind had calmed down, Agnes came to help me wash. Perce went to the village to look after a couple of patients. Agnes and I washed everything in sight. We wanted to start the New Year with a fresh slate. In the midst of the scrubbing and laundering Cyril Okitkun came to ask if the Eskimos could use the schoolhouse for a dance that evening. We said yes, not knowing exactly what it was all about.

When Perce, our communicator, returned in a hurry about six o'clock, he said the dance was especially for us and we should give everyone something as in a potlatch (a giving feast). We didn't have time to bake cookies for one hundred people; so Agnes and I, looking over our supplies, decided on tea, graham crackers, and raisins. We sent Johnny Prince around the village to tell everyone to bring his or her cup.

At six-thirty we rang the bell. Everyone arrived, Paul Yunak bearing his drum. Very quietly, looking at each other, the people sat on the floor around the edge of the classroom. After a silence of about twenty minutes, Roy and four other men came to the front of the room and began to sing very softly. Two masked men went to the center. One knelt with his parka between his legs. This was Cyril Williams. Waska stood. He would imitate what Cyril was doing. They were swinging their bodies and arms to the rhythm of the drum.

The leader of the singers called the names of the songs and told the dancers what to imitate. They sang about their hunting trips, the mountains, birds, fox, bear, beaver, muskrats, and mink. One song sounded like this:

> *E yung e e yung e yah e yah,*
> *e ya ah hu e yung,*
> *e e yah e yung e yah e yah*
> *e yung e e yung e yah*
> *iling lnge hu e yah e yuge*
> *e yung e yuk iling nlge hu e yah.*

The dancers made jerky motions of varying speed with arms, head and trunk to illustrate the song. Frequent short pauses were placed between episodes to provide rest periods and to denote changes in scene. In the dance about a beaver hunt, one dancer stood with bent knees, left elbow bent so that his left hand was in front of his chest, palm toward chest. The right elbow was bent with the hand pointed front. The right foot stamped to keep time with the drummers. Then half-bent elbows were lowered in back of the body, palms outward, back of hands toward hips; the left elbow was raised, the left hand placed in front of the right hand near the navel, while the foot stamped lightly on the floor. This represented going to the beaver dam. Next arms were extended in front with jerky movements as if running, then as if shooting the beaver. The dancer squatted and swayed his shoulders leftward and back to position with wrist movements, while grunting and making various guttural sounds, as if to retrieve the beaver from the water. Music and motions became faster and faster; now fists were closed with jerky movements as if in joy; bended knees went up and down and stamping became faster. The dance ended.

Paul Hunt, the best dancer in the village, recreated an encounter with a black bear he had fought in the mountains. He knelt, every muscle in his body moving to the sound of the drum. At the end of the dance, he fell to the floor exhausted.

Next was a dance for all the men. Each dancer tried to dance better than anyone else, moving arms and bending in all directions with many jumps up and down to the rhythm of the drum. They called to each other, making noises like ducks or animals low in their throats. These sounds and songs were similar to the Klamath River Indians' songs and dances except that the Eskimos moved their bodies and arms more.

Cyril Williams did a dance called, "My Old Aunt Is Asleep." Comically, he went to sleep and woke up with jerks and grunts, swaying back and forth on his knees as if he were having nightmares.

The little boys did a dance imitating their parents. Some did quite well. After the little boys, all the men and women were called by the singers to dance. The men were better dancers than the women but Titinia Hunt danced well and was enjoying every moment of it, obviously flirting with the men.

Last was the potlatch dance. Everyone sat in a circle. The three singers and a drummer were at one side. Each singer had a dry willow stick with shavings curled up on the end of the stick. (This was like the flower stick the Klamath Indians used in the Flower Dance before 1900, when the girls became old enough to marry.) The singers moved their sticks forward and backward in time with the song as two women stood up and danced into the circle. The women seemed a bit bashful; more women were called to join them. The primitive rhythm finally gets to you. I wanted to dance; it looked like fun. One woman was motioning to me to join but I didn't, not knowing enough about their customs.

Now it was time for refreshments. The older school girls helped serve. Everyone wished everyone else a Happy New Year. The fun was over and 1938 was beginning.

The Eskimos had a great love for music and dancing, although their only instruments are a traditional drum and a rattle. They were great singers with fine voices, a sense of rhythm, and a good ear for music. Long before the white man came, they had danced to attract game so that their families might be fed. If they did not dance, the spirits who attended the feasts would be angry and the animals would stay away. Of course, when the white man's religions came to Alaska, some of the Eskimo's beliefs were changed and in places the dances were stopped. I have always wondered why the churches think they know best.

From January second through the tenth there was a siege of flu, colds, and sore throats. Too many social activities and a blizzard that seemed never to stop for more than an hour didn't help matters.

Alex Okitkun, who had gone to Saint Michael with furs for Williams Trading Post, returned and brought us a beautiful coiled grass basket and mat from the Johnsons. They were made by the natives of Nelson Island, who wrapped a number of strands of tundra grass with one strand and kept working them around in a coil until the desired size was obtained. Herb Johnson knew we were interested in Eskimo art and that we wanted to teach the children about that part of their heritage. We greatly appreciated the gift. Immediately we started the girls on coiled baskets. They had already learned to weave large mats. Every household had dried tundra grass which they used at night to cushion the sleeping platforms or beds and to wrap bedding and skins during the day. The mats were also utilized to curtain off the bed, to cover windows and doors in winter, to sit on in kayaks, and in many other ways.

Every day that weather permitted, Perce played football, Eskimo style, with the villagers and older children on the slew in front of the school. The ball was five or six inches in diameter and was made of reindeer hide stuffed with deer hair. Two of the participants acted as leaders. They chose sides until the players were equally divided. At a given distance apart, two conspicuous marks were made in the snow or ice to serve as goals. The players stood by their respective goals and the ball was tossed midway between the teams. A scramble began, to kick the ball across the opponents' goal. Perce slipped and fell, hitting the back of his head. He was conscious but I watched for a concussion. There was no way to get help unless you sent a message by dog team, a five hour trip to Hamilton, where George Butler, the trader for Northern Commercial Company, had a wireless. I worried a bit, but every day Perce seemed better. However, he did not play football for a month.

I began to teach the children to tap dance for exercise and coordination. For creative art, the boys carved wooden masks and small boats to use in their dances and plays. When their faces were covered they danced better and enjoyed it more.

In school we were also drawing house plans for the cabins they would some day build, and making scrap books of useful clippings for future reference. One had to start as in the pioneer days. The village wasn't very far advanced.

I had wanted to walk to the Northern Commercial Trading Post, about a mile from the school at the mouth of the slew, but every time I went to the village the ice was so slick that I fell. Cyril Okitkun saw me and decided to treat my mukluk boots with seal oil. Strange as it may seem I did not fall again, so off we went, Agnes, Elizabeth, Margaret, Perce and I. This was my first trip to the store—not a bad country store. It stocked flour, sugar, rice, tea, and chewing tobacco, canned fruit, and bolts of gingham used for women's outer parkas to cover the skins of the Arctic hare; the fur was worn inside. I bought gingham for two dresses Agnes would make for me. Perce purchased a pair of whip-cord pants. They didn't cost any more than they would have on the mainland. Joe Usiak, who ran the store, showed me some well made coil grass baskets. I bought one to send home to California. On the way back to the school we had a snowball fight. Perce won.

Perce was making daily doctoring visits to the village. He was doing most of the clinical work and enjoying it.

Most of January, there was a blizzard, with the northwest wind blowing the snow in high drifts and the temperature at twenty below zero. I rarely went outside, only to the village when necessary. Nose and cheeks would freeze if one didn't keep rubbing them.

Perce was in the shop putting ivory buttons in tea for the girls' new knitted sweaters. We boiled the buttons in tea to make them look old. Sometimes traders did this and sold the ivory for a greater price. Perce was also teaching the men and boys to carve ivory. They were making knife handles, small birds and animals, and cribbage boards.

Otto Polti arrived with a long account of symptoms that included fainting and blind spells. We advised him to go to Mountain Village to consult the doctor at the hospital. Chiklik, with whom Otto was staying, said he would take him as soon as weather permitted.

Teddy O'Connor, who was bringing mail from Saint Michael, came to us and told us he got lost in the blizzard and almost froze to death. Most of the mail was covered by a snow drift. Teddy's story was a bit vague, so Perce and Johnny Prince took the dog team and went to the creek Teddy had described. They found no trace of his passage or any of the lost mail.

We needed dog mittens to cover our woolen gloves and keep our hands from freezing. Johnny had given Perce his old pair, and Mary Ann was making some for me. When the Eskimos killed an old dog, they skinned it and made mittens with wide cuffs. Strips of cloth or yarn were braided into a cord which was sewed to the mittens and worn around the neck, so that the mittens would not get lost.

The men stopped going to the mountains to hunt fox, mink, otter, and bear because they had very little dried salmon, only frozen black fish to feed their dogs. If they carried frozen black fish on the sled they would have only enough food for two weeks. They would depend on the beaver and muskrat to be hunted in the spring. Perce would go with them on their beaver hunt.

Every family had piles of frozen black fish. The fish were caught in a trap made of thin strips of wood. It was about six feet long, one and a half feet across, and resembled a long, open, woven basket with a funnel at the top. A hole was cut in the ice to fit the trap, which was then inserted through the opening and kept in place by a long stake driven in the bottom of the slew. The black fish, small, like surf fish, about six inches long, would swim into the funnel and could find no way out. There was a door at the bottom of the trap. When the trap was pulled up and the door opened, the fish poured out in a heap and were left on the ice to freeze. That didn't take long at 20 below zero. The resulting mass looked like bunches of black tumble weeds.

Since there was no bakery for a thousand miles, I had to learn to bake bread. Baking was something of which I had done very little. We had brought plenty of dried yeast and flour; I progressed by trial and error. We couldn't eat the first batches of bread. I didn't throw them away, though. The children, who had never before tasted raised bread, thought it great. I could make baking power biscuits and muffins. The trading post had hard tack, but that was a bit difficult to chew. After six months the bread improved. It was not the best, but at least, it was palatable. I even taught the older girls to bake bread.

Mask making delighted the children, so papier mache masks were in order. We started by moulding the mask from clay, then tearing or cutting narrow strips of paper, putting glue made of flour and water on the strips, and moulding them on the clay form. Soon the masks took shape. After they were dry, we lifted the papier mache mask off the clay, and painted and decorated it.

The children were so interested in their projects of knitting, making masks, writing legends and using the library that they stayed at school all hours, until I had to send them home. School was a much more pleasant place to be than their crowded cabins.

Dr. Evelyn Butler, supervisor from the Juneau office, had asked me to write a course of study for a one-teacher Eskimo school, especially Chaneliak. I wanted it to be meaningful, practical, useful, interesting, and to reflect Eskimo customs. It should teach the three R's and bring the pupils to sixth grade reading level, and they should be able to write a legible business or friendly letter. Probably not one child would leave this part of the country.

The boys would stay in school until they built a sled and trained five dogs to pull the sled. This would enable them to hunt and make a living. The girls needed to read sewing patterns and use a sewing machine. Health education would be emphasized, especially in matters of cleanliness, birth, child care, and tuberculosis.

To improve health habits was urgent. Hunts had a visitor from Hooper Bay who had mumps. Now the entire village was infected.

Perce was taking his first hunting trip with Alex. They were going to hunt fox and mink on the flats around Hamilton. They bumped off about 11:30 a.m. in the dog sled, heavily loaded, mostly with dog food. The morning was sunny and twenty below zero as I watched them disappear across the tundra. I expected to have a quiet evening but it didn't turn out that way.

At 4:30 p.m. in came Charley Prince saying, "My wife has baby, baby cry already."

I snatched my grip with the supplies and away I ran. When I reached the cabin door and opened it, I saw the baby in the corner on the floor, lying naked on a reindeer skin. He was covered with blood. The afterbirth had already come away. (How those infants survived was beyond me!) I told Mildred, the daughter, to get a blanket quickly to wrap the baby, while I tied the cord and cut it. Wouldn't you know, I had misplaced my scissors in the shuffle but found another pair and poured alcohol over them. A sterile string was ready in my grip. I tied the cord as quickly as I could and took the baby near the stove. His feet were cold. Poor little guy, he must have been lying on that fur fifteen minutes before I got there.

Pauline, the mother, was old and so fat I hadn't known she was pregnant. I gave them fits for not calling and telling me about the baby sooner. The mother said she was tired and I thought, "You ought to be." She hadn't even taken off her pants. They just had a slit in them so that the baby could slip through. I took off her boots and undressed her, gave her a sponge bath and a clean shirt, then questioned her about the child. Pauline had taken a large dose of castor oil; the baby, Michael, was premature. I made a mental note to instruct Margaret Mary, one of my interpreters, to tell the women not to take any medicine during pregnancy unless I gave it to them.

Then I took the baby, Michael. Usually I just oiled them at first, but he was such a mess that I had to bathe him to get the blood off. I oiled him, put argyrol in his eyes and vaseline on his head, warmed him, put on a clean gown from my grip (Agnes had made several baby gowns for use at birthing.), wrapped him in a blanket and put him in a rabbit parka. I went back to school for the ergot and gave it to the mother to stop the bleeding. Finally I went home, made tea, ate canned stew and called it a day.

The next day after school I bathed the baby, treated the mother, called on Susana, Agnes, and Tom Prince. They all had the mumps. I stopped at Mary Immumik's to tell her what to do if the children came down with the mumps. Mary was ill with T.B. I didn't think she could live very long.

Cyril brought us a hind quarter of reindeer meat. In return, I gave him cans of peaches, pineapple, potatoes, carrots, grapefruit, two cans of milk and some dried fruit. This would last his family more than a week. Their diet consisted of tea, yeastless bread that was fried in seal oil and some kind of fish. Change of season would bring variety, though, ducks, geese, cranes, seals, beluga, or white whale, and salmon in spring, summer, and fall, also cranberries, and willow roots. To obtain the beluga, the Eskimos went to sea in their kayaks in calm weather, paddled along until they sighted a school of beluga and then herded them to a shallow beach with shouts and cries. There the animals were easily killed. The beluga furnished excellent fat food for both humans and dogs.

I went to the shop to tell Cyril to come for his box of food. When I came out the Northern Lights were flashing across the sky making a fan design in the center and casting red rays to the land on each side. Then they changed: a purple light flooded the sky, then white. While I was watching they again turned very red, coloring the snow to match. I hoped Perce was watching. We had never before seen the Northern Lights.

It's strange: the north country grows on one. It is fascinating. It would be lonely though, especially when Perce was away. Particularly at night. However I had plenty of work to occupy me.

In school the children wrote letters to Irving Creek School, in Siskiyou County, California; and to Washington School in Eureka, California, where my sister-in-law was teaching. They received letters in return. How excited they were to read about other children and what they were doing.

I wondered if the Eskimo women got lonely too. One day, making my visits to the village, I stopped at the Prince cabin. Agnes, an old lady, was sitting alone and looking out the window. The cabin was filthy. She could not read but she did sew. Her stitches were so even you would think they were done on a machine. We couldn't converse as she spoke no English, and I little Eskimo.

My medical work took a couple of hours a day; then there were night classes for the women in health and knitting. The book work, which had to be done in detail for the Juneau office, took an hour or more a day. One had, as well, the ordinary chores to do. There was very little time to listen to the radio, which was poor anyway. Sometimes we would get London but no news from the States. So one was isolated from the familar world of home.

In the village one afternoon during Perce's absence, I

met Old Jumbo pushing a sled full of wood she had gathered. She told me her troubles in Eskimo and of course I didn't understand a word. During this conversation a pup ran up to the sled. She took a big stick to him and he ran away whimpering. No one in the village wanted anything to do with her because she was so mean. Since she lived alone and was not sixty-five years of age, I had to ask for direct relief for her. The Eskimos shared their catches and helped one another, but since she was so mean, they sometimes forgot about Old Jumbo.

While in the village, I weighed baby Michael. He weighed 4 lbs. 12 oz., and looked healthy. I stopped at the Hunts: Margaret Mary was tanning a rabbit skin; Ivan's finger was better. (He had cut it while hunting.).

I saw the first baby I delivered, Georgey. He was as fat as a seal.

At last Perce and Alex returned. Perce had enjoyed the trip but had no fur. They had seen two fox but missed. (Most of the Eskimos shot instead of trapping the animals.) The trip had convinced Perce that he needed snowshoes. The snow was still soft and he had sunk deep at every step, making traveling difficult. We would employ old Nick Skaran to make them because he was an expert at making showshoes.

Awaiting Perce was a letter from Hirst directing him to take the census on the south mouth of the Yukon. The government was considering the establishment of a school at Kwiguk. He was also to inquire into the welfare of the Eskimos there and learn how the government money was being spent. Since Alex would be going to Saint Michael the next day to deliver furs to Herb Johnson, Perce would accompany him there in order to pick up the materials for the census.

Angela sent me some frozen berries. I thought something was in the wind, and there was. Margaret Mary brought her to the school and told me she had a pain in her womb. Margaret Mary said, "It has happened. Angela just had to follow her man. She follow him many, many times. Angela will have a baby. Her man is her first cousin. Elizabeth has been with this man too. Father will be very angry."

"What can I do?" I replied. "Father's guardian angel was not on the job. It will be a problem for the Father and the family to solve." They went away unhappy. What could I have said?"

When Perce came home from Saint Michael, he brought Sam Kendrick, the reindeer supervisor, who had been an Oklahoma cow puncher, liked to have a drink, was friendly, easy to talk to and easy to please. He and Perce talked every night until midnight about reindeer, building a corral at Point Romanof with C.C.C. help, how the herd could be increased, and castrating at reindeer camp in the summer. Sam held a meeting with the Eskimos, explaining the rules and plans for the summer. Agnes brought a reindeer permit over to Sam, saying Waska owed her mother some reindeer because Waska had slept with her but eventually married a younger person. He had given the permit for favors received. Agnes requested that someone be appointed to kill two reindeer and deliver them to her mother. Sam told Agnes the permit was not transferable and couldn't be used for that purpose.

The Eskimos slept with many different women. The missonaries tried to change that custom. Like Angela, the women said, "I just have to follow my man."

Sam stayed a week and returned to Saint Michael and his station at Unalakleet. He would return in the summer.

It was a clear beautiful day in February. The last snow had covered the grass except in scattered places where it was peeking out. The white willow bushes were emerging on the level floor of the tundra. You could see dog teams coming for several miles, hauling wood. We had tried to have the people get their wood in the fall by boat or by floating the logs in rafts from upriver to the village, but a few were lazy and never had enough wood.

Simeon brought a letter from the physician in charge of the hospital at Mountain Village. He was sending medicines for us to use, but very little advice or direction. He would make a visit later. He pointed out that the health of the people in the village and surrounding country was our problem. We knew that, but needed professional help. He did give some advice on T.B.; so I called a meeting of the women. I explained one thing over and over, that you ate the germ and the germs were on the dishes; they had to wash and then boil the dishes to kill the germs. Maybe they understood. It was discouraging, but one had to hope they would try to help themselves.

Sometimes I thought the interpreter didn't tell the women exactly what I said even If I repeated the message several times. According to Stefansson and others who had visited Alaska, T.B. was introduced by the whalers who visited the Arctic Coast in the eighteen hundreds. It took a heavy toll of the people due to the fact that the Eskimos had not developed a natural immunity.

Perce and Johnny left with the dog team for Hamilton, Kwiguk, and Akularuk Mission. Perce wanted to meet George and Louise Butler. George was the Northern Commercial Company trader for Saint Michael, Chaneliak, Hamilton, Kwiguk, and Saltery at the south mouth. The permanent company headquarters was at Hamilton. Perce was to question the traders about the government welfare money and how it was distributed among the Eskimos by the Catholic mission at Akularuk.

When Perce returned this was his story of the trip:

"It was 22 below zero; a slight north wind was blowing all the way to Hamilton. Johnny and I took turns riding the sled runners, sitting in the sled and running alongside. We bumped along on the Yukon past Bill Moore's slew, where the Eskimos have their summer fish camp, arriving at Hamilton store at 4:00 p.m. It is a small one room building facing the river, where the boats can tie up in the summer. In the middle of the room was a woodstove with a glowing fire. A couple of Eskimos were sitting, enjoying the warmth. Shelves on three sides were filled with merchandise; a long counter, half-covered with fox and mink furs was on the right. George was behind the counter. He came to meet us with a welcoming hand extended. He is a large man, six feet three inches tall, reddish hair, likes to be macho and brag and blow. He said he had come to Saint Michael in the early 1900s with the Army as a private and stayed after the Army post was abandoned. This was during the gold rush days in the Yukon Territory when all the stern wheelers were going from Saint Michael to Dawson.

"We sat around the stove to talk. I said 'The government has sent me to take the census and to find out how the welfare money is being spent.'

"Most of the money is being spent at Akulurak Mission to maintain the boarding school. A government school is needed, especially at Kwiguk, a village of over a hundred natives, with two trading posts,' replied George. After a few more remarks, Johnny left to feed his dogs and spend the night in the village with friends. We walked back of the store to another house which was the living quarters, where I met Louise and the four children: Mary, fourteen; Marlyn, twelve; and the twins, Anne and Buddie, ten. I had an enjoyable visit and dinner. Louise had a native girl as maid, cook, and mother's helper. Louise taught the children, as there was no school at Hamilton.

"Johnny and I left Hamilton early in the morning. The south wind was blowing; the temperature had gone up to above zero. We crossed the north mouth and headed for Kwiguk. We stopped at the Northern Commercial store. Alex Johnson was running the store at Kwiguk for George. We had tea and dried salmon for lunch, and continued on to Akulurak Mission. By this time the storm had intensified. Snow was blowing in all directions. The dogs were having trouble staying on the trail but we made it, arriving at Akulurak in the evening. I was met by four religious brothers who took me into the kitchen where we had some home brew and dinner.

"Father O'Conner, who managed the mission, came later, He took me upstairs to a small room and asked me not to return to the kitchen. He would be back later. It was like being in jail. Father didn't seem too congenial when I told him I wanted to look at the mission records for the census and to learn who was receiving welfare money and supplies.

"The next morning, Johnny came to take me to visit some of the natives who lived on the tundra. Most of them were old Eskimos. Everyone we visited told the same story. They did not receive welfare because they didn't go to church. They did not believe.

"That night, late, Father came to my room. He had a bottle of whiskey and a box of cigars. We talked all night about the country, caring for the natives, what he was doing for the orphans and the school, but in spite of all his friendliness, he didn't want me to copy his records for the Government.

"After two days of arguing with him, I said, 'Father if necessary I will bring the U.S. Marshal here with an injunction to see the records.' Father did not want the law so he brought the records to my room. In copying them I was surprised to find most of the names were Russian or English. When the missionaries came and the schools were established in Alaska, Eskimos were given these names because the missionaries could not spell nor pronounce the Eskimo names.

"In the meantime Father had taken me on a tour of the mission school. There were four nuns teaching the children. They gave me pictures of the school and a needlepoint the children had made to take home to my wife. My business completed, I was happy to get started back to Chaneliak. On the way back we stopped again at Hamilton. Mrs. Butler gave me a beautiful coiled tundra basket to take home to you. I was glad this trip had ended."

Perce had many jobs with little pay. He spent many hours on the census, which included people in a radius of five hundred miles. There were reindeer reports: although the books showed thirty thousand on the range, there were only twenty-five hundred when counted. Maintenance on the buildings was endless: the old stove pipe was forever falling off, the classroom full of smoke from that terrible Alaskan coal.

Health clinic was held every day. Ambrose's baby teeth hadn't fallen out, so he looked like a shark. Pulling his extra set was all in a day's work.

There was shop work everyday. The two sixteen-year-old boys, Alex Hunt and Tom Prince, had finished their sleds with Perce's help and trained five dogs; now they were ready to hunt. It was time for them to graduate.

Everyone in school was having a grand time reading and rewriting Eskimo legends, then revising them into puppet plays. The boys were building a stage. The girls were dressing the puppets and making stuffed animals. We were to have the program for Eskimos near and far in early April before muskrat season opened.

On Valentine's Day, the weather had turned warm; everything was thawing. Water was dripping through the roof on our food supplies and down into the classroom. The ice cream I made, the children didn't like. Our party was a wet one. Then it turned very cold, 50 degrees below zero, and all the medicine bottles with liquid froze and broke. So between the thawing and the freezing, we were in a bit of a mess. Our reindeer meat thawed and we gave it to Kamaka, the medicine man, and his family.

In the first part of March, Father arrived from Stebbins for a few days; so I had a chance to practice on the church organ for our program. Because of another warm spell, the ice on the slew was melting and it was difficult to get across from the village to church or school; so Father loaned us a dory. Perce rigged a pully so that the children could get in the dory and pull themselves across. This was great fun. They wanted to do this all day, but we had rules.

Dr. Evelyn Butler and her husband, Dale, also a supervisor, arrived by plane. He continued on to Stebbins village. We were very happy to see Evelyn for we needed her help and advice. She had been in the village only a few hours when Anne Okitkun had a baby girl, so she saw me in action and she helped with the delivery. Afterward, we visited all the houses, made sick calls and saw Joseph, the crippled boy. Evelyn said he would get welfare.

We went to Kotlik with Alex by dog team. Mary and the baby were well, but John, her husband, was dying from tuberculosis. While Mary was serving us tea, we instructed her to boil the things that John used in order to keep herself and the baby healthy.

After we left Mary, we went to make other calls. We saw Angela and her baby. Evelyn noticed how much cleaner Kotlik was than Chaneliak. The natives were more industrious and had larger caches of food.

During the return trip on the sled, we talked about improving Chaneliak. It could be made a cleaner village by putting down boardwalks and improvising dog houses of oil barrels dug part way into the tundra at a distance from the cabins. Wooden floors should be washed after seal, mukluk or beluga had been cut up in a cabin.

We talked about a temporary summer school at

Kwiguk; tent platforms and tents to be sent to Kwiguk for school and community meetings. The field nurse and I would spend the first summer in makeshift accommodations and the second summer we would have the tents. This way, the Juneau office would know if a permanent school was needed. We continued talking most of the night until I lost my voice. In the morning, Perce and Evelyn went over plans for the school building including oil stoves instead of coal and wood, a dispensary where the children and women could bathe. In their cabins there was no privacy.

Evelyn could see how much I needed the field nurse, Alma Carlson, so she promised to make arrangements for her to come and stay a month or more with us.

In the afternoon, we entertained Evelyn with selections from our projected program, a puppet play and a dramatization of one of the legends. The girls also did a tap dance. The small boys had a drill on the cock horses that the older boys had made in the shop. Evelyn asked that I send some of the puppets and the plays to the Juneau office after the community program.

The plane arrived at 4:00 with Dale. With his movie camera, he took pictures of the boys doing Eskimo dances in the masks they had made and of the girls with the puppets.

The entire village had come to see the plane take off. Everyone was happy and smiling. As we said our goodbyes, the plane soared into the cloudy sky and we were alone with our Eskimos.

Since our meat had thawed and we had given it away, Perce had been hunting ptarmigan with Alex, but without much luck. The last trip, Perce shot three: the dogs ate two and he gave the third to Alex. Ptarmigan are something like grouse or California mountain quail and very good eating. On Sundays since the snow was melting, the women and children would take a sled with three dogs and walk on the tundra to Kotlik or Pastolik gathering moss berries left from last fall. They had been frozen all winter in nature's ice box and everyone was hungry for fresh berries. A foot of water was standing on the small lakes on the tundra. Everything in the village was wet, dirty, and muddy.

With the warmer weather, the doctor from Mountain Village arrived. He was young, starchily professional, and eager to take pictures. He photographed seal skins filled with seal oil. Hanging outside the cabins, seal stomachs blown up like balloons to be used as spear floats caught his attention. (When hunting seal in open water, the Eskimo tied a float to the spear; when a seal was hit, the float prevented it from diving).

Every cabin he visited was cutting up seal. In Paul's cabin, a huge wooden dish made from a log five feet by three feet had a dead seal in it. Irene was sitting on the floor carving seal meat and placing it in the dishpan.

She was using a curved knife made of slate with a wooden handle. It looked like a food chopper. Margaret Mary was sitting on the floor stretching seal skins from which the hair had been removed and preparing them for water boots.

Paul had five rabbit skins drying on the wall to use for Margaret Mary's parka. He was eating the largest plateful of boiled black fish I had ever seen. Our next stop was at Johnny Prince's. He had a large carbuncle which we had been treating. The doctor put iodine on a swab and ran it around in the cavities of the carbuncle. I thought Johnny was going to faint.

After snapping more pictures, the doctor was ready to leave. Walking was difficult in the soft snow. Alex took us to the plane in his dog sled. The doctor was on his way back to Mountain Village.

On April eighth, we presented our spring program. Dressed for the occasion I put on my white high heel shoes. How strange I felt after six months in Eskimo boots. At 7:00 p.m., with the sun still shining, I rang the bell and the audience, some seventy-five adults and children, filed in. The school children did their parts well, except Ambrose, cast as a baby bear. He cried and didn't say a word. The puppet plays were a great success as was the tap dancing to the tune "Turkey in the Straw." The evening ended with enthusiastic applause.

The next day the girls washed the sheets we used for curtains. They had soap suds all over themselves and the classroom. They had a hilarious suds fight. I didn't stop them; they deserved a bit of mischief.

On April fourteenth the children reported excitedly that they had seen the first seagull of the season. All the birds, ducks and geese would be here soon to nest. Several dog teams were leaving to spend Easter at Saint Michael, where Father would have services and entertainment. I made plans to go with Alex on his sled. This was my first long trip away in seven months.

I wrote reports and made the list of supplies needed for the following year. The list had to be in the Seattle office in time for supplies to be put on the August boat for Saint Michael or we would have no food for the following year. Puppets packaged, mail ready, I was packed and happy to be going. Last of all I had to put seal oil on my Eskimo water boots. I hadn't worn them lately and we would be going through water and wet snow.

When Alex and I left at 6:00 a.m., the temperature was forty above and a slight northeast wind was blowing. Cyril's team caught up with us. We were neck and neck all the way to the cabin at Point Romanof. We had kept close to shore because the ice was melting on Pastol Bay and ice was thickest near the shore. With the thaw, water was everywhere. It would be break-up time soon. The Yukon would be open and there would be boats traveling up and down the river. It was 9:00 a.m. when we reached the cabin. We had tea, Alex fed the dogs blackfish, then we went on. We trotted along past the point. To the east, the mountains were capped with snow. Alex sat beside me on the sled and told me the names of the mountains and of the various slews.

Cyril's team was just a speck far behind us, and we had a glimpse of Charley Aparezuk and George Komaka ahead of us. After riding on Norton Sound for a couple of hours, we went up on the tundra. In places the snow was entirely gone. The ground was ready for birds to build their nests and lay their eggs.

We bumped along for two more hours then reached the canal. Aparezuk and Kamaka were there. With them were two of my pupils, Elizabeth Kamaka and Mildred Prince. The girls were exploring the old river boats beached in the canal. In the paddle wheel of one of the boats was an old crow's nest. The crows stay all winter. In a few minutes Cyril's team came along, bringing Alex's daughter, Mary, to join us. We ate dried fish and drank tea. The Eskimos told me they appreciated my sharing their food and not eating provisions I had brought for myself, as whites usually did when traveling with them. "When in Rome do as the Romans do," had always been my motto.

I took some pictures while the men changed the little boots on their dogs' feet. The boots were made from heavy canvas, reindeer or seal skins. In the spring the sharp ice cut the dogs' feet. The boots wore out quickly; so the men carried several sets and changed them when needed.

All four teams started at once. You never saw or heard so much howling and running. The wind blowing in my face and the miles of country stretched ahead reminded me of horseback riding. Looking across the ice of the Bering Sea, I thought, "How strange to be here. Soon the ice we are riding on will be water flowing to all parts of the world."

The canal was thirteen miles from Saint Michael. We crossed the tundra for six miles and came to another canal. As I was tired of sitting on the sled, Alex and I changed places. Riding the sled runners, I felt the wind smarting my face. Once in a while the sled runners would hit a hole, plunging my feet in water. Five snow-white hare scurried away as they saw us coming but stopped at a distance and looked back. I was enjoying every minute of my ride. As we were nearing our goal, I again changed places with Alex. At 5:30 p.m., we reached Saint Michael. Father was there to meet us. I went directly to Mrs. Johnson's. She saw me coming and was drawing hot water in the tub for me to have a bath. What a luxury!

On Saturday I met Payne, head of the Civil Conservation Corps. At his direction the natives were tearing down old barrack buildings. Sometime in June, lumber would be sent to Chaneliak by barge to build sidewalks and a dispensary for the village. The dispensary would provide a place where the women and girls could take baths.

There must have been three hundred natives in Saint Michael for Easter Mass and the festivities. What a mass of color with all the women and children in their bright parkas! Mrs. McCarthy, the teacher at Saint Michael, was helping with the games and races. Mildred Prince won the sack race. She would have a happy story to tell her mother and all her friends when she arrived home. Mrs. McCarthy had invited us to dinner after the festivities. She had made wood fiber flowers for favors and decorations.

Everyone was making us feel at home, even Herb Johnson. He was a strange one, up at three-thirty every morning and sometimes too crafty for his own good, always trying to make a buck but helping everyone where he could and an excellent storyteller. He and I discussed providing fish nets for our natives so they could catch more fish in the salmon season. I ordered ten new nets. The natives would work for us, helping Perce build the dispensary and sidewalks to pay for the nets.

Tuesday, getting ready to go home, I realized that twelve hours on the sled had played havoc with my skin. I was severely windburned; and now I had twelve more hours to go. We left Saint Michael at 6:15 a.m. The dogs started running fast. I almost fell off the sled. Paulsen's and Kamaka's teams were running neck and neck with our team, but we soon fell behind. We reached the canal with the old boats at 9:00 a.m. Alex fed the dogs blubber. Leaving the icy canal we ascended the bank. Reaching the tundra with a hard bump, Alex almost broke one of the sled runners. As a change from riding on the sled I was trotting along keeping up with the dogs. There was no sign of life except one red fox and a few old crows.

We reached Point Romanof just at twelve o'clock. The teams belonging to Aparezuk, Paulsen, Kamaka, Cyril Williams, Roy Hunt, and Cyril Okitkun all arrived. There were eight teams in all. You never saw so many dogs on one beach howling and fighting.

Mildred, Mary, Elizabeth, eight men and I crowded into the shelter cabin to have lunch. We had dried salmon and pilot bread, and I treated them to tea and cookies I had bought at Saint Michael. The men grabbed most of the cookies as if they had never before seen a cookie. While the girls and I went down to the beach to see what we could find, the men split wood and made kindling for the next travelers who would stop at the cabin.

The men joined us there and fed their dogs; then we

were ready to start on the last part of our journey. Roy was the first, acting the clown, yelling at the dogs, and jumping up and down on the runners. Cyril Williams was second and we were third. Mary Okitkun, Alex's daughter, was riding with us. We went like lighting over the broken ice, through the water and finally caught up with Roy. He had a large dead mukluk and three small seals on his sled, which was old and had no brakes. When he wanted the dogs to stop, he pulled with all his might at the back of the sled, yelling "Whoa," but it did little good; the dogs raced on. He dropped his dark glasses in the water. As I had an extra pair, we came alongside his sled so he could snatch the glasses I was holding out to him.

As we traveled on, there was a great deal of water on the ice; one side of the sled broke through the ice and Mary and I almost rolled off into the water. Alex grabbed us just in time. By this time we were getting close to Chaneliak. I could see the telegraph poles at the Northern Commercial store. The wind was blowing at my back. There was no backrest on the sled.

Charles' and Cyril's teams were to the right of us. The dogs were trying to bite each other. Charles was hitting his dogs with a dog chain and running alongside them to keep them untangled from Cyril's dogs while Cyril's sled was bumping into Charles' sled. It was the end of a twelve hour run for the dogs. They were very tired of pulling on the same side and had to be changed around. Each team consisted of an odd number of dogs with one at the front as the leader and the others hitched behind in pairs. Cyril finally pulled his team to a stop and switched three of the dogs to the opposite side. Charles went on to the village.

We were the third team home. Getting off the sled in the village, I plodded across the slew through water, a very tired, windblown person. Perce was waiting at the front door of the school. I was mighty glad to see him. I had enjoyed the experience but was glad to be home.

Father came the next day from Saint Michael and went to Kotlik for a dory, which he carried back on the sled for use in crossing the slew to school and church. There was so much water on the ice that we needed the rowboat. Perce put it in the water and fixed a pully system to draw the dory back and forth across the slew. The children thought this a great game. We had to put a stop to their dangerous play. The ice was breaking up and moving around in the slew. It could crack the dory, or the children might fall in the water.

A few days later Perce went on his first seal hunt with Alex. This was his story as he told it to me.

Three dog teams left Chaneliak early one spring morning, with Pual Yunak, Chiklik and Alex driving. The old medicine man, Keyoria, went along as their weather man. Alex said Keyoria always knew when the northwest wind was going to change. A southeast wind would carry them out to sea. The medicine man rode with Chiklik and was his partner. On Alex's sled were two kayaks, a small tent, mats of tundra grass to put on the ice under the reindeer skin sleeping bags, guns, and a primo stove that burned alcohol for cooking. Their food was hard tack biscuits, dried salmon, seal oil, and tea. Tea is an important beverage for the Eskimo. He can survive for days on the food mentioned if he has plenty of tea.

They jogged along on the bumpy ice for thirty miles to open sea on Norton Sound. After pitching their tents they had tea with biscuits dipped in seal oil and watched for a seal, with guns in hand, on the edge of the ice, now about six feet thick. The tide was coming in and Alex saw a seal's head. He fired; all three men jumped into their kayaks with their harpoons, paddled as fast as they could, and when they reached the seal that was thrashing in the water, threw their harpoons at the seal's body. Chiklik missed but Alex and Paul hit dead center. Seals thrash in the water for about five minutes before they sink. Floats prevented the harpoons from being lost. The harpoons were about eight feet long, the head being barbed and fitted into a socket at the end of a shaft. A line was attached to the head and fastened to the shaft in such a manner as to make the shaft into a drag when the head, imbedded in the animal, became detached. The head was ivory or bone, the line a thong. The float was an inflated seal's stomach attached to the shaft. Their seal was a big mukluk seven feet long. Alex towed and dragged it up on the ice and cut out the liver. This was a great treat. They ate it raw; it was warm and tasted like cooked liver. Perce joined in the feast.

Alex divided the mukluk with the others. He and Perce were partners, so they had first choice of the best part, the front quarters, because Alex had shot the seal. Perce said he didn't want his share of the seal meat, but that was a big mistake. Alex scolded him when they were alone and told him to take his part because he was his partner and then give it to him later. Alex shot two more smaller seals. Perce knew better now and took his share.

Chiklik killed one, but Paul was not lucky. All day long Keyoria would stand around and look at the sky and test the wind. On the third day about 2:00 a.m., he woke everyone up and said, "The wind has changed to the southeast. We must go; the ice will be breaking up." They packed in a hurry and returned home. One could land in Siberia on an ice floe.

When the men arrived home, Alex's wife, with her curved knives, would cut the seal's mouth wider, go inside, and pull out the stomach and guts. If there were whole shrimp or small fish not digested in the stomach, the family would eat them. The guts would be split lengthwise, cleaned, then sewed together and made into a rainproof parka for her husband.

Father had come back to Chaneliak after Easter. I was practicing songs in the church every day for our program, scheduled for the last day of school before summer vacation. I was glad the church was on the same side of the slew as the school because the ice was melting fast. Father said I should close school on May fifteenth but I decided on the twentieth.

On the last day of April, Perce was getting ready to go beaver hunting with Alex and Waska. We got up at four a.m. and had breakfast. Perce went to the village to help load the sled. I couldn't go back to sleep, so I read a while. About six I looked out the window and there were those three fellows in front of Waska's cabin. Of all the comic sights! Perce was pushing the sled with kayak and camping equipment heaped high on it. Alex and Waska were pulling with all their strength, while Waska's old reindeer dog, tied on the side of the sled, pulled backward instead of forward. They had finally started to move forward when huge hail stones began to fall; so they had a splendid send off from the skies. After the hail stopped the heavy rain began. I was glad Perce had remembered to take his slicker.

The children were tired of school. The older ones wanted to set their muskrat traps, hunt ducks and geese and rob their nests. This was the only time of the year you could have fresh eggs. They would be available for three weeks until the birds formed in the eggs.

Joe brought me a goose and a duck. I had just finished picking them and had feathers from one end of the house to the other, when Father sent over another goose. He wanted to be asked to dinner. I decided the next time I had birds to pick, the girls would do it. They picked them clean, clear up to the head so that only the eyes were looking at you. We needed the feathers for stuffing dolls and a pillow.

Perce had been gone for three weeks on his beaver hunt. Every day Tom Prince, my oldest boy in school, took his spy glass, stood on the top of one of the log houses in the village and looked toward Pastolik to see if Perce was walking on the tundra on his way home. On Saturday, May fourteenth, Tom came running over to school to tell me he could see Perce walking and Alex coming into the slew from the Yukon in his kayak. It was late afternoon when Perce arrived; he looked like old Father Time. He had a beard, needed a bath and had lost twenty-five pounds. He was packing five skins of beaver he had shot, four large and one small. We kept the small one for Mary Ann to make me a pair of short winter boots with beaver skin tops.

Perce had had a successful trip and had lived like an Eskimo. This was this story:

After their start with the sled and dog, the three trudged along pushing the sled east toward the mountains. The tundra was slippery and wet. They stopped at Pastolik for tea and rested until night when the cooler temperature made for better traveling. Chiklik, Paul Yunak and Steve Immumik joined them at Pastolik. After three days and nights of travel, the six of them reached the Andreafsky River where the mountains began. They left their sled and kayak, carrying their reindeer sleeping bags and supplies on their backs. Five feet of snow was still on the mountain.

Thirty miles of hard traveling up hill and down gullies brought them to the beaver dams where they made camp. Waska and Perce were partners. The first day they saw several beaver eating on the willows. Perce was first to kill one; the others scattered. Returning to camp with the beaver, the men skinned it. They prepared to stretch the skin by making a hoop of willow sticks the size of the skin. Holes were punched an inch apart around the edge of the skin through which to thread fish line which was then tied to the willow hoop. After the fat was scraped off, the skin was stretched tight and left to dry.

If the beaver had been feeding on light willow bark, the meat tasted like very fat pork, but if it was eating dark willow bark, the meat was very bitter. Perce wouldn't eat the bitter meat, but the Eskimos did. They boiled the bitter meat and dipped it in seal oil. Perce fried the legs of the beavers that had fed on the light willow bark.

After hunting late in the evening and early in the morning for ten days and living on beaver meat, rice, flour doughcakes fried in seal oil, and tea, Alex decided they had better return or he could miss buying many beaver skins from other hunters for Frank Williams' Trading Post. Besides they had no more food. Perce had a little rice left in an old dirty sock, but would you believe it, after Perce cooked it Alex wouldn't eat it, as unsanitary as he was. Perce ate it, there was nothing else and he was hungry.

With the snow falling, Alex and Perce started back, but the other hunters stayed. The snow underfoot was still frozen at night. Alex thought he knew a shortcut that would bring them home in two days. After a day and a half, they looked around and saw some of the same beaver dams they had passed two days before; so they returned to the old trail. Perce lost his footing on the slick snow, dropped his gun and he and the gun slid several hundred yards to the bottom of the hill. Finally, they reached the Andreasfsky River where they had left the kayak and sled. Alex would kayak home on the slews and rivers. He told Perce to walk straight across the tundra, using the masts of the old sternwheelers at Pastolik as his guide. So he walked and walked all day and night. When he reached Pastolik, one of the Eskimo women fed him a whole boiled goose; nothing had ever tasted so good. He had walked thirty miles in twenty-four hours and was glad to be home. Tessiani was haivng her first baby and making a big fuss. She wanted the entire family, Father, and me with her. Margaret Mary and Father's interpreter, Margaret Koka, were with her most of the time. I kept going over every few hours but the water was so high I was a bit frightened to stay too long. Leaving instructions for the two Margarets, I went home at midnight. At 2:00 a.m. Koka came for me but couldn't wake me, so she said. Father came in the morning and said the baby, a boy, was born at 2:00 and everyone was well. He had the two Margarets in the church sleeping; they had been up with Tessiani for three nights. When I went to see her everything seemed under control: Margaret Mary and Koka had taken good care of her and the baby.

However, all the jabbering in Eskimo which I was having trouble understanding convinced me that something was wrong. I didn't want to be involved in Tessiani's problems that didn't concern the birth. She had been so frightened although the other women giving birth had been so calm, even when they had lost their babies. I couldn't understand it until one of the women told me Tessiani was flirting with other men and she didn't want the baby. It didn't belong to the man she married. This was Father's problem, not mine, so home I went.

Our first year of school was almost over. We cleaned the desks. The children took home old Beacon readers and magazines to take to fish camp. I was hoping they would read during the summer. The girls were getting ready for a big picnic. Agnes and Koka made yeast bread; Alma, cake; Mary, cornbread; Mamie, cookies; Elizabeth, candy and nut bread. You can imagine what my kitchen looked like. We made May baskets and filled them with candy and cookies.

The last day of school arrived; the weather was windy and rainy. We had our program of singing, games and picnic inside. Everyone who was in the village came. It was a happy day. The next day Agnes came to wash for me, and the other girls, to clean the classroom and kitchen, but water was still at a premium. There hadn't been enough rain to fill the barrels; so we used the slew water. I would have to do my own laundry and cleaning soon when all my girls would be at the fish camps.

Perce was appointed to tag beaver. Many natives from surrounding villages were coming to school to have their beaver tagged. Perce ran out of tagging material. About that time Otto Polte appeared from nowhere with his boat. Perce sent him to Hamilton with a wire to the game warden for more material.

Records were to be done and books balanced. It seemed I spent as much time on the records as I did on teaching and health care. George Butler arrived for a short visit. He took my records to wire the Juneau office. He had a boat with a powerful motor; with the ice gone on the Yukon and all the waterways open, he could make it back to Hamilton in two hours. He had come to ask us to visit his family since Louise, his wife, with Mary and Buddy, their two children, were leaving soon for Seattle. Buddy had contracted tuberculosis and needed medical attention; Mary was entering high school. The two younger children were to stay with their father until the end of the summer, when they too would join their mother and attend school. For several years, Louise had been teaching her children with the help of correspondence courses sent out by the territorial school at Juneau. Now it was time for them to go to a real school. Perce was unable to accept George's invitation because of tagging the beaver, but I accepted. On May 28, Joe Usiak, Steve Immumik and I left Chaneliak at 10:00 a.m. in a small dory with an outboard motor. As the tide was high we could enter the Yukon. We circled around the mouth of Chaneliak slew and into the river, where we bounced along on the waves watching many types of bird life. The terns were darting and whistling overhead with the seagulls; the snipes and egrets were running along the shore; there must have been twenty different species of ducks feeding on the north side of the bank. Steve, with his single-shot twenty-two, shot at the ducks but didn't hit a one. We reached Kotlik about eleven-fifteen. Baby Agatha had a cold and fever. I gave her baby aspirin and left medicine and instructions for Mary, her mother, then had coffee with Mary's mother and her husband, Stefan Kamoroff. The mother couldn't speak a word of English; but I managed to make signs. We all laughed and enjoyed our visit.

We returned to the dory; and as Joe started away from the village, he almost cut up a whitefish net with the boat's propeller. Seeing it just in time, he swung the boat around in a big circle. Steve was standing, lost his balance and nearly fell into the slew; but we missed the net and away we went into the main river.

Whitefish are as large as salmon. The natives depend on them for food in the spring before the salmon arrive. They are good eating if you skin them; otherwise they have a strong oily taste, not very palatable.

The country near the mouths of the rivers for miles and miles was nothing but small slews and lakes. George Butler told us a true story of a teacher at Akiachak on the Kuskokwin River who was going to Bethel in a small dory, taking one of the supervisors from the Juneau office. There were so many slews that he got lost and went around and around for two days, until they realized they were passing the same fish camps and waving to the same natives. They came out near Akiachak where they had started. So one had to know the river. We learned always to take a native with us if we were going any distance from the village, summer or winter.

As we traveled along the river we began to see flocks of geese feeding and flying overhead. Most were Canada geese, but we saw a flock of emperor geese on a sandy beach. We slid the boat quietly toward them. Steve, with his little pop gun, was ready. He shot and wounded one. Jumping out of the boat, he started to run after it. The goose wasn't slow in running either. They had a regular race on the beach: the goose running and honking, Steve hopping and running on his short legs as fast as he could go. In the end the goose lost because it could not fly. Steve's shot had broken its wing. Steve and Joe had goose for dinner.

When we arrived at Hamilton at three-thirty, all forty inhabitants of the village were on the bank with Mr. and Mrs. Butler and their four children to greet us.

I went up to the house with the Butlers. Joe and Steve, carrying the goose, went with friends. Butlers' home was a large log cabin. A combined kitchen and livingroom, two bedooms and a bath were downstairs. The attic had bedrooms for the children. Lucy, an Eskimo woman, helped Louise. She was treated like one of the family. She had been with them since the children were born. Lucy had roasted a sand crane for dinner. It was like Thanksgiving. George had just returned from Black River and Kwiguk where he managed trading posts. Since we were tired from our trips, we retired early. Tomorrow would be Sunday.

When we awoke for breakfast, the two older children and friends, six in all, were preparing their lunches to go egg hunting. They were having a great time laughing and deciding what to fix. Finally they were ready. Joe was taking them in George's high-powered boat because the sky was cloudy and the river rough. George was afraid to trust Mary, his oldest daughter, with his boat in bad weather. Fresh eggs were such a great treat!

For three weeks after the ducks, geese, seagulls and other birds arrive to nest, their eggs can be eaten. Seagull eggs are especially good, just like pullet eggs. After three weeks, the baby bird is formed in the shell. All eggs shipped from the States are paraffined.

We ordered two cases, sixty dozen, once a year. After three months, they were a bit strong and we used them only for cooking.

The children came back without eggs. The birds had hidden their nests well. To help with the diet, the Butlers had a vegetable garden: greens and rhubarb grew very well there in the summer, in contrast to Chaneliak on the tundra.

On May 30, a beautiful day with no wind and the sun shining, it was time to return home. Mrs. Butler got out her camera and took pictures of us leaving.

On our way back, Steve sighted a flock of geese and ducks feeding along the shore: I had never seen so many in one group. Landing the dory, Steve was sneaking up on them when three geese flew toward the birds on the beach and away they all flew. They circled higher and higher in the sky until we could hardly see them, making many different formations, first a big "V," then two small "v's," then another big "V" with two small "v's" on each side.

All at once, the small "v's" flew off and landed on the tundra.

On we went, drifting slowly down the river with the motor turned off, not to disturb the birds. We rounded a turn and saw two cranes doing their mating dance. It was a strange, beautiful sight. One bird would jump up and down, then pick something up in his mouth and throw it at the other bird as if he were playing ball; then he would leap high in the air and flap his wings. This was repeated many times.

Steve said if Eskimos sing their native songs to the cranes, they will dance a long time. I wanted Steve to sing, but he wouldn't try.

We reached the store at the mouth of the slough about 3:00 p.m., where we changed to a smaller boat because the tide was out. When I arrived at the school, Perce was just finishing a meal of seal liver. I was hungry so I joined him. It is just like calf liver.

We shared our experiences of the past few days. Perce said Father had told him how he was training Margaret Koka to be an interpreter, housekeeper, and assistant. We laughed a bit because Father had picked the wrong young lady. She had a temper, was not pleasant to others and was stubborn. Of course, he might frighten her into submission, since we were finding out this was the way he persuaded the Native people to attend Mass every morning before going hunting. He would show them slides, purgatory and the devil, then tell them they would go to hell if they didn't attend Mass.

We did not approve of this and told Father he was to discontinue showing the slides. Our relationship was waning.

All the people in the village, including Father, were painting their boats, to put them in the water. It had been windy and cloudy for a week and 45 degrees above. The rains had come as well as hundreds of swallows, building their nests under the eaves of the shop and schoolhouse. They flitted by the windows all day long. One came out on the porch to sing to me as I was brushing my teeth. If one didn't have human company, the bird life made up for it this time of year.

Perce had been cleaning and painting the shop inside and out, painting the desks and cleaning everything in sight. There was no darkness now and the natives had no sense of time. They ate when they were hungry and slept when tired. At midnight, I saw the brightest rainbow in the northeast I had ever seen in my life. This country was awesome.

Father came to get the organ he had loaned me and to talk about our five year plan for the village. The plan was ready to send to the Juneau office and he wanted to read it.

Now that the ice had gone out of the Yukon, boats were arriving in Saint Michael from the States. From Seattle, Frank Williams had arrived with his boat, the *Meteor*, which had the mail contract from Saint Michael to Kotzebue, going through the Bering Strait and stopping at villages along the way.

One of the first freighters was stuck in the ice off Nome and the steamer *Columbia* with four hundred passengers, was due there in a few days. We were going on the *Daisy* to Saint Michael to help unload frieght for the villages around Norton sound and the lower Yukon. All the freight for over 20 villages was unloaded at Saint Michael and put on smaller boats to be delivered to its destination.

The wind had been causing problems for some of the crafts, but with Perce's help, Alex put the *Daisy* in the water as well as all the Eskimo boats, large and small, in our village.

We left Chaneliak at 4:30 a.m. on a beautiful day except for the wind. At reindeer camp, we stopped on a sandy beach. Everyone was glad to see us, especially the children. I had gum for them and Perce had leaf tobacco for the adults. Alex delivered flour and picked up muskrat skins; then we were off again into the Bering Sea headed for Stebbins to deliver Father's organ.

When we arrived at Stebbins, it was 3:00 p.m. The teacher, Mrs. Perrian, invited us to the school and began telling us her problems. The children didn't come to school most of the time. The parents ignored the problem and her. The men made and drank sourdough. I told her you couldn't teach school as we had in the States. One had to see the needs of the native people and make up one's own curriculum and activities. But she had decided to leave Alaska in August.

The wind had picked up. As we left Stebbins, the *Daisy* was rolling this way and that, but we made it to Saint Michael by staying close to shore. I was a mess, tired and dirty. Being on one of the small native boats with no water except for drinking, no toilet facilities except a three pound coffee can and no sleep for seventeen hours wasn't much fun.

Nell had my bath ready and then dinner. Herb was busy with the barge. Henry Trager and Gladys, his wife to be, were at dinner. Gladys was taking the *Columbia* outside to the States but would return in the fall to marry Henry. They were a pair: both tall and skinny, Gladys nervous, a clinging vine with her arms around Henry, talking like a magpie, Henry looking embarrassed but giving her a kiss now and then.

Henry was Charley Trager's nephew. He had come to Unalakleet to help his uncle at the trading post. Charley was getting old and Henry was to take over his responsibilities. Henry was a trickster, too, playing tricks on anyone he could. Once he had stolen George Butler's eight cases of beer off the barge bound for Hamilton. Perce was in on that prank.

The insurance company paid for lost freight, so they figured George wouldn't lose. Henry then tried to steal Perce's four cases (which Perce had put in a gunny sack) by sending one of his deck hands to the guest house for the sack. Perce was there, so that trick didn't work. The only way anyone got alcoholic beverages was to have them sent in by plane or boat. Naturally there was a bit of swiping and trickery among the white traders where liquor was involved.

Henry had brought the *Tex*, his launch, and a barge from Unalakleet for the freight off the *Columbia*. No one had received freight for nine months. One received supplies from June through August while the Bering Sea was open for travel. Herb, Henry, and Perce were very busy hauling goods from the *Columbia* and unloading it on the shore at Saint Michael.

Gladys was packed and ready to leave; so Nell and I went on the *Tex* with her to board the *Columbia* and spend the day visiting with teachers and other friends we had met on the *North Star*. Nell had met the teachers when the *North Star* was in Saint Michael when we arrived in October. The teachers were going outside for summer vacation.

It was midnight before Herb, Henry, Perce, and the crewmen had all the freight unloaded from the *Columbia*. Nell and I had enjoyed visiting, and having lunch and dinner. We said our goodbyes relunctantly.

We were put back in the cattle box that had hoisted us aboard. I wasn't so keen on the way the cattle box was swinging around in a circle over the sea and we were being knocked from one side to the other. Finally, we were lowered and stepped out of the box onto Herb's launch.

Perce and Henry were all over the sound hauling freight to different villages. Everyone was tired. Herb hadn't slept for thirty-six hours; so he went to bed and I went down to the shore to direct the unloading of the last barge.

The natives weren't too happy to have a woman boss. What a mess, freight everywhere! I had the natives separate the river freight for the *Ensee*, the Northern Commercial boat, run by Captain Holsher during the summer months.

The *Ensee* went from Saint Michael up the Yukon to Marshall, also called Fortuna Ledge. A dory and two outboard motors, one five-and one ten-horse power, were in the pile of freight. Now we would not be so dependent on Father and the natives; the dory and motors would be on the *Ensee* the next trip up the river. I worked eight hours at the unloading. The natives got used to a woman boss and we got the job done.

As the Bering Sea was rough for three days, the crew had a rest. On the fourth day, the freighter *Oduna*, which had been anchored behind Egg Island, as well as three other waiting ships, the *Meteo* from Wales, the *Ensee* from Hamilton and the Coast Guard cutter *Northland* came into Saint Michael Harbor. The *Northland* made regular stops at Saint Michael to give medical help. I had wired the ship while it waited outside the harbor, to make an appointment with the doctor for a physical. Dr. Edmundson, the physician, was accompanied by the field nurses, Mrs. Edmundson and Miss Shepherd. Their first task was to attend to the health needs of the natives. I helped Mrs. Edmundson gather up the patients—children and adults— and boarded the ship. The medical group worked all day caring for the sick. The next morning I had my physical. Dr. and Mrs. Edmundson came to Nell's for lunch; Herb even took time off to eat lunch and socialize. The *Northland* and *Oduna* sailed in the afternoon.

When the *Ensee* sailed up the river, we would return home. Captain Holcher was in charge of the Northern Commerical boats, the *Ensee* and the *Mildred.* He was seventy-two, a nervous little man, and sometimes ran off and left his passengers. We hoped we wouldn't wear out our welcome at the Johnsons; so we would watch carefully when the *Ensee* was ready to sail.

Frank Williams left to meet the Bergin freighter and unload mining equipment. He would take it up the Unalik River.

Sam Kendrick arrived with his wife-to-be, Joyce. This was her first time in the north. She wanted to explore Saint Michael; so I took her to Pat Sweeny, the marshall. He admitted us to the old Russian church and escorted us through one of the stern-wheelers that was still intact. We went to the Northern Commercial trading post, where we saw two carved ivory tusks from Nelson Island. I still think I was a chump not to have bought them for $10 each, but money was scarce in those days.

The day was sunny as we boarded the *Ensee* at 9:15 a.m. The boat would not leave until 11:30 but we wanted to make sure we wouldn't be left behind. The Klondike barge was still being loaded. We saw our dory, the motors and some of the lumber for Chaneliak. They would unload at the trading post at the mouth of the slew, and Alex would bring our supplies, dory and all, to the schoolhouse.

Opposite reindeer camp, we stopped for the tide until 3 a.m. There was plenty of time to visit. Captain Holsher told us he was to be married later in the summer and showed us his fiancee's picture. I wonder if I would care to marry at such an advanced age. One never knows. About 4 a.m. we arrived at the trading post on the point. Joe Komegan brought his dory and we rowed up the slew with clouds of mosquitoes following and biting, but we were protected with head nets and gloves.

July passed quickly. Perce painted the inside and outside of the shop, the desks and everything else that needed painting. He took the old banking away from the school building so that new timbers could be placed under the building: thus it wouldn't look like a boat. Then he insulated the floor.

Since we had our rowboat, which we named the Loon, Perce would row up the slew nearby to kill ducks and geese. The natives, when they came from time to time to store their dried salmon at their homes, brought us fresh salmon, which I canned.

Father, the game warden, or other travelers might stop on their way to Hamilton if the tide was in, but most of the time everyone passed us by as they traveled up the Yukon.

The tempo of our lives picked up when we prepared to go to reindeer camp. I would accompany Perce while he took part in castrating, branding and enumerating the animals.

Before the white men arrived in Alaska with rifles, wild reindeer in abundance had ranged the tundra and the coastal mainland north of the Alaska Range. They were used for food and their skins were made into parkas, pants, footwear, bed covering, tents, and sails. After firearms were introduced the natives slaughtered reindeer wastefully. By 1880 there were few left. In 1892, through the efforts of Sheldon Jackson, first chief for the Office of Indian Affairs in Alaska, tame reindeer were brought from Siberia, with herders and their dogs, to relieve the food shortage of the Eskimos. By the early 1900s the white traders had bought up most of the reindeer herds.

At one time Lowman Commercial Company had refrigeration and was shipping reindeer meat to the States but the venture was a failure. In the 1930s the government began to buy the reindeer back from the whites for the Eskimos. Herb Johnson, the Eskimos, Perce and I, under the direction of Sam Kendrick, reindeer superintendent, were to have a reindeer roundup. Its purpose was to count

(Left) Allen, my only first-grader at Petersburg. (Below) Student body, Petersburg.

(Above) Perce on the *North Star,* "That nasty Alaskan coal" in the background. (Left) From left to right, Bush, the ship's jester; Clarice Kerr, my shipboard friend, and another officer.

(Above) Drying salmon at fish camp. (Below) Castrating reindeer at reindeer camp, near Chaneliak.

(Above) Chaneliak family. (Below) Louie, my little organist, with his father, Steve, and little brother.

(Left) Mike and Justine, parents of the premature twins.

(Above) Elizabeth Kamaka at Point Romanoff. (Below) Tea break near beached stern-wheeler on our trip to Saint Michael.

(Above) Father Lanneux, Bishop Fitzgerald, and native population of Chaneliak. (Below) Dog team on the Yukon.

(Above) Our comic, Roy Hunt, standing, and family. (Below) Andy
Hunt with the sled he built for his graduation project.

(Above) Leo and Leah making a kayak in the school shop. (Below) Alma Prince with her mother and brother inside their cabin.

Ptarmigan with little George, my "first baby," and Tom Keys with his children.

(Left) School children at Chaneliak, with their papier mache masks.
(Right) Joe Aparezuk, Tom Prince with Joe's mother, little George and a blackfish trap.

Mamie robbing a mouse nest of roots.

A puppet play at school.

Picnic lunch at fish camp.

Filleting fish to dry.

(Above) The *Ensee* and Klondike barge. (Below) Stewart, engineer on the *Mildred,* with his wife.

(Above) Evening health meeting at Kwiguk. (Left) Teacher and students at Saltery summer school. (Below) Returning to Chaneliak after summer school.

(Above) Pupils at Kwiguk with author and Alma Carlson. (Below) At
Kwiguk, even pre-schoolers attended.

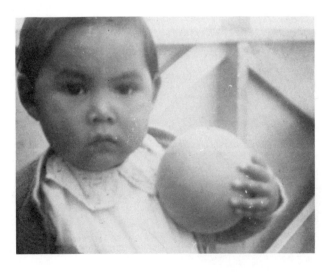

(Above) Living quarters at Kwiguk. (Right) Eskimo mothers at summer school meeting. (Below) Home-made school furniture.

(Above) Rock wall at Skagway, bearing inscriptions by Gold Rush miners. (Below) Stuart Widener, holding the youngest child; Kathryn, second from right, and Perce, right, battling mosquitoes. We were leaving Marshall, Alaska.

and brand for government purchase the animals owned by Frank Williams, which made up most of the herds around Saint Michael and Chaneliak.

In late July, we had everything ready for this undertaking. Perce and I were going to camp on the *Daisy* with Alex, Ulrick and several other Eskimos. The *Daisy* arrived at 3:00 a.m. with a load of dried salmon to place in the Eskimos' caches for winter. The sun was just rising on the horizon with its hues of red, orange, blue, and purple; the wind was blowing slightly, just enough to keep some of the mosquitoes away. This was a splendid morning to be traveling out to sea. We left with the tide. Alex stopped at fish camp to pick up his tent. As we were approaching reindeer camp, we saw something white offshore. It was the *Warrior*, Herb Johnson's boat. We came up close and anchored. The *Warrior's* engine had been taking on water, so Herb had it all apart. He gave us his tent, which was on board, asking us to pitch it near the corral. We got into the dory and rowed toward the shore. We could see a little white streak way out in the sea. The boys said it was Sam's boat coming in to camp.

At 9 a.m. we began to pitch our tents. We made coffee, had lunch and spent the rest of the day dealing with camp equipment and preparing for the arrival of the herds. After Sam had anchored his boat, he rowed to shore and got Perce to go with him to Chaneliak for oil for Herb's engine. While they were gone a high tide came in and almost took our tents out to sea. By night everything had calmed down.

Herb got up early and went out to work on the engine. I sighted Sam's boat returning. The natives brought salmon and cranberries for the lunch which I was preparing for Perce and Sam. The third day, Perce and Sinka, who was head herder for Williams, had an argument about the corral. Perce didn't think it was strong enough to hold the reindeer. Sinka didn't want to fix it because Williams hadn't told him to do so but Perce prevailed and the corral was repaired. No deer had been driven in yet, so Tom Okitkun and Perce walked to Coffee Point, about three miles. They brought back a mammoth tooth. Little did we forsee the interesting future that tooth would have. After our return to Chaneliak, I used it for a bookend in our library. A couple of years later there would be a huge explosion and frightened children were screaming. When we looked around to see what had happened, we would find the tooth in hundreds of small pieces. Apparently gas inside the cavity expanding in the warm indoor air was sufficient to explode the tooth.

It was cold and raining, with nothing to do. Feeling the need of exercise, I took a walk on the beach. I hadn't gone far when I met a porcupine. It showed no fear. It would stop as we were strolling along, sit up, sniff the air, look at me as if to say, "Who are you, invading my territory?" Finally I turned back and watched him plod along the beach until he was out of sight. I should have had my camera.

Late the fourth day, Sinka, Alex and others came into camp with the herds. As the deer arrived the men made a long line about thirty feet back of the herd and walked along slowly to drive them into the corral. Some were milling around counterclockwise. They were hard to persuade, but finally we broke up the milling and got some into the corral.

The next morning everyone was up early to put the deer through the chute. As a deer came out of the chute an Eskimo would bulldoze it by grabbing its long horns. With very little struggle the deer were castrated, branded and let go. We worked the herds for two days, but no more deer arrived. We had handled around three thousand animals.

A gale with heavy rain swept in. Herb's boat broke anchor and drifted to Coffee Point, With the engine out of order, there was no way to control the *Warrior*: it was driven on the rocks. The waves pounded the boat, knocking it against the rocks and making a hole in the bow. Sam was so worried about his boat during the storm that he beached it. Herb took Sinka's boat to replace the lights on the blinkers at the mouth of the Yukon which had been blown out during the gale. In the meantime Alex took the *Daisy* to pull the *Warrior* off the rocks so that the hole could be patched and he could tow the *Warrior* to Saint Michael.

Our stay at reindeer camp was over. We were returning to Chaneliak on Sam's boat, when again the weather changed; the air was calm. As we entered the slew, huge black balls of mosquitoes filled the air and seemed ready to devour us. We finally docked in front of the school. Sam and his two deck hands stayed until the next tide, when they left for Saint Michael. Our adventure with the reindeer was over.

Sam was disappointed that there were so few deer left. Perce was not too surprised, as he had seen many deer carcasses left to rot, with only the tongue removed. In such remote, sparsely populated country, the source of this depredation remained a mystery.

Most of the time we were alone in the village except for the coming and going of the natives bringing their dried fish and wood for the winter. There was nothing but daylight now and a great deal of rain. Sometimes I took walks on the wet tundra wearing my big shoe paks. With the temperature at 45 degrees and a slight wind blowing, it was a pleasure to walk in the brisk cool air. The prettiest blue flowers, like blue bells with a leaf like a columbine, were growing everywhere, as well as the wild iris. The banks were alive with color: yellow daisies were going to seed and Alaskan cotton—something like dandelion fluff—was covering the tundra.

Our friends from Unalakleet were sending us fresh vegetables. Our diet was getting a big boost with fresh fish and fowl: we were living like kings.

On the *Ensee* at the end of August I made another trip to Saint Michael for jacks to raise the building and more lumber and nails. Nell was in Unalakleet. Frank Williams, his son Bill, and Herb were batching; so I took over the household chores.

The *North Star* arrived at Saint Michael on its way to Point Barrow with our personal supplies. If you didn't order everything you needed or wanted from the States for the following year for delivery via the *North Star* in August, you did without.

Charles was up to his old tricks and gave me a fine sling ride to the deck in a net. I was wrapped in the net like a sack of potatoes, safer than on my previous trips standing on a flat platform and clinging to a rope.

Claude Hirst was aboard. We had a long visit about the summer school I wanted to start the following year. I had refreshments with the crew and then was tossed back in the sling by Charles.

The steamer *Denali* came into harbor and anchored. Captain Holsher was busy with the *Ensee*, pulling loaded barges to shore from the *North Star* and the *Denali*, and I was riding back and forth with him, taking no chances on being left at Saint Michael. He loaded the covered *Klondike* barge last with our supplies and all the other freight for the Yukon and we were headed for the river. Eight hours later, as we approached the north mouth of the Yukon, the fog was thick. Captain Holsher was afraid to go further than the trading post near Chaneliak, so he decided to beach the *Klondike*. It was better than watching a circus, the boat going this way and that, the captain yelling at the deckhands; but finally they landed and started unloading.

The deckhands had used planks to make a ramp from the barge to the tundra so that they could unload freight for us and the trading post.

Captain Holsher had started to walk up the plank when he slipped and fell about five feet onto the tundra. He hit his head on the plank, was shaken up, had bruises and a cut on his arm. I thought it best for him to come to the school and have his arm bandaged while the barge was being unloaded.

About the same time, Pete Jorgensen's small boat come chugging through the fog. Beside Pete and the deckhand, were Perce and Father. The four men lowered the dory and rowed over to get me. Taking Captain Holsher and his nephew with us, we rowed up the slew. By the time we arrived at the school it was 7:00 a.m. Breakfast was in order. Everyone was hungry. It was customary, indeed necessary, to lodge and feed everyone who arrived at the village whether you knew them or not.

After breakfast, with Captain Holsher duly bandaged, he, his nephew, and Pete returned to their boats. Perce now had enough material to start the improvements on the school building. He hired a Civil Conservation Corps crew made up of men from our village. On August 29, they jacked up the building and began to repair the floor. Cyril Okitkun, the best carpenter in the village, put new windows in the school room, kitchen, and upstairs storeroom. (Sometimes the upstairs was invaded by shrews that packed our extra boots full of beans and rice.)

Stairs were built to the store room to replace the ladder. The kitchen was equipped with cupboards and new wall board, and shelves were installed in the classroom. A room, ten feet by fifteen, was added on the front of the school for a dispensary. It would contain bathing facilities for the women and children as well as storage space for our medicine. Sidewalks and bridges made of wooden planks were constructed in the village. Anthony Keys built a log cabin with Perce's help. Anthony and Alma Prince would be married.

Alex left with the *Daisy* on August twenty-first for Mountain Village Hospital with sick adults and children. There had been an outbreak of pneumonia and several deaths, including Angela's, while the families were at their fish camps. Alex returned on September sixteenth with his well patients, medicine and instructions for us from the doctor in Mountain Village.

III. Old Hands Now

I had already started school on September sixth in the church because of the improvements going on in the school building. Margaret Koka Hunt was now working for Father so was not in school; but all the other families had returned to Chaneliak for the winter and my children were happy to be back in school.

Frank Williams came on October eighth with the last of the supplies needed for the building. From Nell he also brought me Rusty, one of Fanny's pups, a reindeer dog descended from some of the original herders' dogs brought over from Siberia with the reindeer.

The same day the *Ensee* was making its last trip down the Yukon before freeze-up. Father and I went out to the boat to get the mail and to meet Captain Holsher's bride. She was small in stature, friendly, but might not wear well in the rugged north. Almost everyone was home in the villages. One doesn't travel the Yukon when the shores are frozen and the ice is forming on the river. We had the first snow on October eleventh. It didn't stay on the ground; but from then on, there was snow or rain every day and the Yukon began to freeze over.

To my surprise, about one o'clock on October twenty-sixth, with a light snow falling, I heard an outboard motor. Going outside I saw a small boat turn into the slew. As it came closer I could see that Alex Johnson from Hamilton was driving George Butler's powerful outboard. With him in the boat was a large woman wearing a parka over striped coveralls, lined, I later learned, with Arctic hare. This was Alma Carlson, our government field nurse, who was to become a close friend. Alma, who was Swedish, was called one of the "three war horses of the north." Clarice Kerr and

Miss Keaton were the other two. These three nurses traveled and took care of the medical and dental problems of the Eskimos north of Unalaska pass. Alma's territory was the lower Kuskokwin, Hooper Bay, Nelson Island and the lower Yukon.

I was happy to see her. Now I would have professional help for my Eskimos. Alex brought in her gear and immediately started back for Hamilton. He didn't want the boat to be frozen in the Yukon or damaged by the ice.

The next morning we were up early. Alma was ready for a full day. Snow was falling, the temperature was thirty degrees above zero. Dismissing the children, I became the student. We visited every house in the village.

Alma said she expected everyone at a meeting that evening in the school, where she would explain her work at Chaneliak. At the same time she was observing the health conditions, which we would discuss and hope to improve.

Everyone was at the meeting, men, women, and children. Mamie, my best interpreter, repeated in Eskimo as Alma spoke. Alma told them she would examine every man, woman, and child in their homes and would do one or two families a day. There would be clinic and classes for the women in the afternoons. The men would have night classes twice a week.

School was held in the mornings while Alma went to the village to examine the families. In the afternoons the women and older girls came to classes. Mamie again was interpreter. Alma started teaching prenatal and child care. She trained three mothers and two teenage girls for midwives: the women: Margaret Mary Hunt, Anna Okitkun, Monica Prince; the girls, Margaret Koka and Agnes Keyes.

We had demonstrations of assisting at birth. Agnes, who was seventeen and about to be married, acted as the pregnant woman. It was like a comedy with all the heavy breathing, laughing, and Eskimo "jabbering." Despite the commotion, Alma was an excellent teacher. We were all learning valuable lessons and enjoying every minute of it. In class we furnished a small baby trunk to be used at time of birth with all the supplies needed, such as sterile scissors and string. Two of my older school girls made baby clothes and flannel blankets for the box. Alma demonstrated the use of the supplies. To have all needed supplies handy and clean would be a great help.

We had had ten deaths in a year, some from premature births and others from tuberculosis and pneumonia. Since tuberculosis was prevalent, Alma next concentrated on prevention of contagion. Tuberculosis had been introduced by the whalers in the 1800s. The Eskimos had no natural immunity against it. In the women's classes, the mothers were told not to chew food and put it into babies' mouths. She explained how the tuberculosis germs were eaten and in this way infected the babies. She told how the women could enclose the sick bed with curtains so others in the family would have protection from the coughing, spitting, and breathing of the infected person. Written materials were given out, which were also used in teaching the children.

In the evening classes, Alma asked the men to add a room on to each cabin housing a tubercular person, explaining the advantages for the sick person and for those in the family who were well. Steve and Rudolf started their rooms. Sadly, it was too late to help Steve's wife, Mary; she was in the last stages of her illness and would die in a few months.

Alma showed them how to take care of cuts and wounds. The men made medicine bags of unborn seal hair and reindeer skins to pack medicines they needed on their hunting trips. She talked to them about caring for their children and advised them to use less tobacco for themselves, their wives and their children. Murdock had reported in 1892 that the practice of chewing tobacco was common; even little children were seldom without their "cud," frequently of enormous size.

Perce once threw away a half-smoked cigarette while in the village. Little Ambrose, a first grader, grabbed it up and chewed it. He did get sick; so he didn't try that again.

We gave out pills in small metal boxes. The Eskimos would use these boxes for chewed tobacco after they had taken the pills. They chewed leaf tobacco, mixed it with ashes, spit into the pill boxes and chewed it over and over again.

Several of the men had boils due to poor diet. In Chaneliak there were almost no vegetables or fruits. The

Eskimo diet consisted almost entirely of fish and meat. There were, however, low bush cranberries and moss berries growing on the tundra. In the fall my school girls and I would take our lunch and in our motor boat would travel to other parts of the tundra to gather cranberries as well as pieces of willow and other roots the mice had stored under the moss for winter. Walking along on the tundra, we looked for a small, soft, raised place, then with our forked wooden tool, we lifted the moss, folded it back and uncovered the nests where the roots were hidden. We robbed the mice of their winter food. The roots were boiled or stored for future use. I tried the boiled roots and they tasted like bitter potatoes, once was enough. However, in some parts of the north like Unalakleet, the ground is fertile and many vegetables were grown in the long summer days.

It was getting close to Alma's departure. Five families from Kotlik arrived and Alma worked three days examining them. The women and men of Chaneliak were having their last lessons. The men brought in their medicine bags to be filled and to have their last visit with Alma. Their bags were very well made with compartments like a purse, and lined with flannel.

Alma and I made plans to meet at Hamilton after the ice on the Yukon went out. We would travel on the *Ensee* to Kwiguk on the south mouth of the Yukon where we would spend the next summer together, traveling to the fish camps, teaching and helping the natives.

George Butler was in charge of trading posts at Kwiguk, Saltry, and Black River for Northern Commercial Company. Bluff, blustering George with his outrageous sense of humor, had totally overwhelmed Miss Carlson, "warhorse of the north" though she be. She refused to visit him alone at Hamilton; so I was enlisted as a chaperone, paying an overnight visit while she examined the three families at Hamilton. In a way, I couldn't blame her, the crazy things he would try!

One time when Perce was with George at the store, George was bragging about how much money he had; we knew it not to be true. He threw three hundred dollars in the stove. Fortunately there were only a few warm coals, and Perce pulled the money out of the stove. Then George laughed and thought it a big joke. What a guy! We couldn't help liking him.

After twenty-one days with us, Alma left Chaneliak for Saint Michael, riding on Joe Usiak's sled. Eleven dogs with paper roses tied on the harnesses pulled the sled. It looked like Christmas. Away the dogs trotted over the ice down the slew, everyone in the village waving goodbye. I was loooking forward to working with Alma during the coming summer.

During the winter, entertainments were an important part of village life. At Halloween we had a party for everyone, including Miss Carlson. The older children made masks of papier-mache' and the younger children made masks of paper bags. We wrote a Halloween play. It was about the old Eskimo custom of having a patron, which was an animal, fish or bird that watched over an individual and saw that he or she prospered. The children acted the parts of their patrons and made costumes and masks.

Mary Okitkun was a loon; Anna Okitkun, a seagull; Louis Imumik, a seal; Maria Aparezuk, a whitefish; Maggie Prince, a muskrat; Joe Aparesuk, a bear; and Tom Prince, a mink. They imitated their patrons by making noises and gestures, by dancing, and being as amusing as possible. They succeeded and the audience roared with laughter.

We had a "fish pond" full of gifts, which was a great success. The girls had wrapped everything we didn't want around the place, extra canned goods and cereal, old magazines, books, clothes, rice, beans, and flour. They also packaged cookies they had baked. After the program and games, came the Eskimo dancing. How they loved their dancing! They stayed until I sent everyone home. They would have danced all night and the next day.

Since Father would not be at Chaneliak for Christmas but at Stebbins, he moved his Christmas entertainment to Thanksgiving. Appropriately, he prepared a mock "giving feast."

Before the white man had arrived, an Eskimo village, some time during the winter, might invite the inhabitants of a neighboring village to a giving feast. The hosts would take months to prepare, learning the dances and songs before even inviting the guests and the festivities would take place in the *Kashim.* Valuable gifts of seal skins, seal oil, even kayaks were presented to all the inhabitants of the guest village. When the first traders came the host village could be in debt to the trader for years. The chief might spend as much as a thousand dollars at the trading post. The average income of an Eskimo man was $500 a year or less. The missionaries discouraged the giving feast because at times the hosts would give everything away and have nothing left for themselves.

We were told the story of a wiser host, the chief at Saint Michael. Frank Williams, the trader, attended the feast. The chief asked Frank what he wanted. Frank said, "I want a boat like the Victoria," which was in the harbor at the time. The chief thought a minute, reached in the cigar box and said, "Here is a dollar and a half. Go buy yourself one!" Frank often told this story. He thought it a great joke on himself. Eskimos have a lively sense of humor and enjoy playing tricks on one another.

Father Lonneux' "giving feast" involved only Chaneliak and the villages nearby. The women were hosts, the men the guests. Father gave all the gifts, as he had done the Christmas before, clothes, blankets, cloth, and toilet articles.

Before the festivities the men left Chaneliak with their dog teams to go to the Yukon and wait. At 2:00 p.m. the two runners, Alma and Mildred, were sent out wearing wolverine head bands and carrying willow welcome sticks. They gave a welcome stick to the first team and received matches in return. Starting back to the village they met two more runners to whom they gave their head bands and sticks. These runners continued to the Yukon, then turning back to meet the next runners. This went on until all the men had been welcomed to the feast. The chief woman, Margaret Koka, fed the visiting chief first, offering him anything he desired. The guest wanted *acuta,* which was blubber mixed with seal oil, bush cranberries, fish, and reindeer meat. (This concoction was called Eskimo ice cream. After the traders arrived, if no berries could be found, raisins were sometimes substituted.)

When the chief had been fed, all the other men were given food. Then the chief woman began to dance and presented the visiting chief with gifts, telling him in song how wonderful and valuable the gifts were, just like a traveling salesman. As she danced, she held two little carved wooden heads with white owl or ptarmigan feathers. Up and down she moved her knees, arms and hands, swaying her body gracefully. At the same time, the drummers sang and kept time for the dancer.

Then all the adult women got up to dance and gave gifts to the men, the visiting chief naturally getting the most gifts. Then it was time for the men and boys to dance. Waska danced first, showing off and doing the Russian dance as well as the Eskimo dance. Each man did his dance, telling his hunting story and acting out the part of an animal he had shot or that got away. All the boys danced at one time, some trying to imitate the dances their fathers had done. Last of all, the women and girls danced. This ended the feast.

For this, our second Christmas, on the last trip of the season the *Ensee* had brought us a small pine tree from upriver. We wouldn't have a skimpy willow as we had the first Christmas. The older girls made woolen jackets for the children eighteen and younger from the long coats Father had given us. Eskimos use jackets for summer wraps and under their parkas in winter. So we found a use for the long coats Father had been saving for years. Patterns and zippers had been ordered from the States. It was a happy day at Christmas when every child had a precious new jacket, besides wooden and stuffed toys, knitted gloves, mittens, socks, and scarfs. (I had taught the women and girls to knit.)

The boys had made medicine chests and door stops for their parents with Perce's help. The door stops were needed especially in summer to let the fresh air into the cabins.

I had contacted the Red Cross, and they had sent each child a Christmas box containing toilet articles and a toy. In appreciation we sent the Red Cross two Eskimo dolls the children had made with carved wooden heads and cloth bodies stuffed with reindeer hair. The girl doll was dressed in a calico dress, an Arctic hare parka and fur boots. The man doll wore felt overalls, gingham shirt, fawn skin parka, and sealskin boots.

Christmas was a gay affair. Everyone sang Christmas carols. Dressed in costumes, the children told the story of

Baby Jesus. Roy Hunt, the comic, was Santa Claus, teasing everyone as he gave out the presents. All the natives were dressed in their Sunday best, women with new cloth dresses and parkas, men in new overalls. It had been a profitable fox and mink season. Each man had shot ten or more animals; so it was time to dance and play.

With Father gone, there were no church services, but there was much activity in the shop making sleds and kayaks. The whole population of Chaneliak and the nearby villages danced every night from Christmas to New Year; and on New Year's Eve at midnight, there was a shooting and shouting good time.

The school house was one big clubhouse. Winter programs were very much in demand. I had a festive Valentine program with hearts everywhere. We decorated with red and white crepe paper, made fancy valentines sprinkled with snowflakes, served more cookies and raisins, and of course, danced. On Washington's and Lincoln's birthdays we dramatized our history lessons with stick puppets, and the adults were our audience. It all helped to make the season a little less dreary.

Then the winter set in with a vengeance. Temperatures bounced up and down. The southeast wind blew; there would be high tide and water on top of the ice, with the temperature above freezing. This went on for two weeks. Then the northeast wind would blow a gale and the children had to be escorted across the slew by their fathers lest they be blown down and injured.

The weather was taking a toll on health. Even Perce was ill after helping the mail plane take off. The tail of the plane had frozen into the ice. At the back of the plane, Perce was shaking the tail loose, and ice was flying in his face. He contracted a strep throat. He was out of his mind for several days. His throat was so swollen I had to keep steam-irrigating his throat twenty-four hours a day. I sent a message by dog team to Hamilton for a plane to take Perce to Mountain Village Hospital, but the weather would not let the plane land; so I did the best I could and he improved. I realized then how isolated we were and without help.

It was frightening with so many deaths in the village. Perhaps the saddest was Mary Immumik, who left four small children. Louis, eleven, was her eldest and was gifted. He knew nothing of music, but, hum a tune and he could play it, chords and all, on the little organ, his short legs pumping as hard as they could go; while I had to practice hours to play a simple tune. I was a bit jealous.

Perce and I were doing more nursing than anything else. Isidore Hunt, one year old, had pneumonia with a temperature of one hundred and four. We had just received penicillin. We cut the tablets in fourths and went across the slew to the Hunt cabin. As we entered we saw many burning candles and people on their knees saying the rosary in unison. At once we stopped the praying, sent people home, blew out the candles, opened the door to air the room and gave Isidore one-fourth pill of penicillin. Perce continued to give Isidore one-fourth pill every four hours for two days. On the third day the child was playing and running around the cabin with no fever.

Strange happenings occurred during that bitter winter. Many deer were found dead with only the tongues taken. People blamed the wolves; so Sam Kendrick, reindeer superintendent, flew in for a few days to help. The pilot would fly low over the wolf pack and Sam or Perce would shoot from the plane into the pack, killing many of them.

Perce and Waska went hunting by dog team several times with little luck. Thinking a new gun might help, Perce bought a 30–06 from Northern Commercial Company for sixty-three dollars. Cyril Okitkun wanted Perce's old 30–30. Eskimo fashion, Cyril said to Perce, "You have a new gun. You don't need the old gun, so you should give it to me. I don't want to pay for it, because you don't need the money." This didn't please Perce; he demanded thirty dollars for the gun. Finally Cyril said he would haul ice for us in the winter by way of payment.

With all this bad weather, we were lucky to receive mail once a month and even then, the pilot would fly over and throw the sack out on the tundra or leave the mail at Hamilton. We would get it when one of our natives would be up that way and bring it to us. The pilot wasn't going to get stuck in the ice again and we couldn't blame him.

I had commencement on March twenty-ninth. Three of my older boys, Tom Prince, Joe Aparezuk, and

Andy Hunt had made their sleds and trained their five dogs for hunting; so they graduated. Three of my girls were old enough to be married; so I had six to graduate.

But the girls were having problems with their men. Jane came to talk to me. The people in the village were saying she was in Cyril Okitkun's house too much. I said, "Marry Teddy, the sooner the better." Then Father came over to tell me Teddy was getting cold feet and didn't want to marry Jane because she was seen running away from Cyril's cabin at night. I was wondering where Cyril's wife Anna had been all this time. Few there lived without sex and variety; and here I was pushing Jane on Teddy. Then Alma, who was ready to marry Anthony, was in Cyril's cabin. Cyril decided it was about time for him and Anna to move to Pastolik and hunt muskrat. I was thinking too many girls were involved with Cyril. He didn't seem that attractive to me, but the girls seemed to like him. Teddy reconsidered and slept two nights with Jane. (There is more than one way to catch a man.) Alma slept with Anthony.

They had a double wedding and Father was happy. After the wedding they came to the school and I gave each couple the following for a wedding present: four pounds of lard, a ten pound sack of corn meal, two cans of peaches, cigarettes, two bars of soap, two cans of cleanser, and a package of macaroni. They all went away in a happy mood.

Perce had helped the people for two years, making many improvements at school and in the village. After we talked the matter over, he decided he should go to Nome for the summer to get a job with the U.S. Mining and Smelting Company. He needed another job since he was making only fifty dollars a month as a government helper. I would stay at Chaneliak until it was time for Alma Carlson and me to go to the villages on the south mouth of the Yukon to teach and nurse the natives.

Jack Jeffers and his sister-in-law flew in with the mail on April eighth and stayed two nights. How I enjoyed Marie's visit! I caught up on all the war news and happenings at Unalakleet and Nome. The newlyweds, Henry Trager and Gladys, were very happy running the trading post at Unalakleet. They were looking forward to seeing me in May on my way to Nome where I would visit Perce before going to the south mouth of the Yukon. Jack and Perce made plans for Jack to pick Perce up at Saint Michael on April twentieth or twenty-first and fly him to Nome.

Perce left Chaneliak by dog team with Alex on April nineteenth at six-thirty in the morning. I just hated to see him go, but we both thought it best. I knew I would spend many lonesome nights with only my dog Rusty for company. My days would be busy though. In the village we still had many ill with flu and pneumonia. When Alex returned from Saint Michael, his baby son Theodore was ill. Alex brought the thermometer over to show me: Theodore's temperature was one hundred three. I told him he should have told me before his trip that the baby had been ill. He was a bit huffy and didn't seem to care if the baby lived or died. I didn't think the child would survive long because he was born a blue baby with a heart conditon. His twin sister had died at birth.

At once we started for the village. A forty mile gale was blowing. I thought I would never get there. The snow was in my eyes and all over me: even my underwear was wet.

The baby was worse. Rosie, the mother, hadn't done a thing to keep him warm. So I stayed, made a warm flannel jacket for him and fed him warm water and orange juice that I had brought with me; but the poor little fellow didn't have much strength. Rosie and the two grandmothers who were there got on their knees and said the rosary. After the prayers one of the grandmothers showed her appreciation by sewing my rabbit parka that had a tear in it, and the other grandmother wiped my boots. I had worn my short beaver boots, since we had been in a hurry, and they were caked with ice and snow.

With baby Theodore dying, Alex had to go out in that terrible storm to gather firewood left by high water along the banks of the Yukon. Men in our village never had enough firewood for the winter. It didn't seem important to them. They were too busy fishing and hunting the entire year to think about firewood. I stayed at Alex's all day and part of the night to care for the baby, returning home about midnight.

Rusty had missed me and had been naughty, chewing

Perce's slippers to bits. I knew how he felt: he must have missed Perce too. I hoped Perce and I wouldn't be separated again. It was too lonesome.

Theodore died the next morning. It was a sad and lonely time. I went to the village to help with the burial. The wind was still howling. The snow was blowing on the ground while the sky above was blue and clear. It seemed as if the earth were burning with the white smoke boiling up to devour the buildings. As the snowdrifts grew higher one would have thought we were in the middle of January.

Still the people were coming from the villages for medicine. Old Jacob brought me a slate Eskimo knife that had been used before they had steel knives. It was shaped in a half circle. He must have liked me to give me his old knife.

During the storm late that night, I awoke to a loud banging at the front door. Rusty was barking. When I opened the door there stood the Eskimo, Big Head, from Stebbins; he had come fifty miles in the storm with carved ivory for me to buy. He wanted cash to purchase a gun out of a Sears catalog. He knew we were the only ones to have real money besides the trader, who would only give him tin money to spend at the trading post. Big Head carved beautifully. He offered a pair of salt and pepper shakers. The salt shaker had a seal carved on each side; the pepper shaker had a walrus carved on the front. There were four small ivory charms in the shape of bears and seals and a bracelet carved with a ptarmigan in the middle, two walrus, two fish, and two fox heads on the sides. The bracelet is the most exquisite piece of ivory I have. I gave him forty dollars for the lot, and he went happily on his way.

Before the storm abated, the widower Steve returned from Akulurak Misssion, where he had taken his children. He talked for an hour. He told me about his trip. He thought the children would be happy. One of his dogs had died in the storm. Steve had stopped at Hamilton where George let him sleep in the store and fed him. I didn't know he could say so much in English.

On May fifth I left with Alex by dog team for Saint Michael, where I would board the mail plane for Unalakleet, then go on to Nome. Several other teams were traveling to Saint Michael to sell beaver, mink, and fox skins. We left Chaneliak at 5:00 a.m. A fair wind was blowing from the south, but within the next hour the weather changed and it began to snow heavily and drift on me until I was soaked and miserable. I packed down under the canvas on the sled, but I was already wet. The snow melted on my ruff, dropped inside my parka hood and ran into my ear. My toes and fingers felt as if they were frozen. When we reached reindeer camp, I said to Alex, "Stop! My parka is wet, I need to thaw out. We can build a fire in the cabin."

Alex drew the team to a stop and there was Sinka, just arriving with his team. The three of us climbed a big drift and dug our way through snow and through a broken door into the cabin. Ice was piled around the stove but the men got the fire started and I began to dry out. Chiklik arrived looking like a snowball. Paul and Gus arrived all wet. We stayed an hour and a half until everyone was a bit drier.

The weather had cleared and only a light snow was falling, but I had learned my lesson: I got down in the sleeping bag with the canvas over me. I was as snug, "as a bug in a rug." Rusty had run alongside the sled all the way from Chaneliak, but now that he couldn't see me he jumped on top of me and rode on the sled too.

Reaching Point Romanof at twelve-thirty, we went into the cabin to warm up and have tea. What a mess! The cabin was littered with cans and looked as if it hadn't been swept for a year or more. We didn't stay any longer than it took to have our tea.

On the sled I bedded down again in the sleeping bag with the canvas over me, Rusty on top again, much to the disgust of Alex. Dogs should run and work.

As we neared Pikmiktatik and the cabin where we were to spend the night, I could see several mukluk pokes filled with seal oil and skinned muskrat meat suspended outside. Entering the front shed, we saw two reindeer carcasses hanging with some of the meat cut away.

This would be my first experience staying overnight in an Eskimo cabin. We were unexpected; we stopped because of bad weather.

When you live in Eskimo land you do as the Eskimos

do. I had dried salmon, tea, and raisins to give to Old Lady Lupon, who greeted us and had the water boiling for tea. We were served hot tea and Eskimo bread. It was gratefully received. She then busied herself by sewing on a hunting bag for her husband. Her daughter was working oil into a white rabbit skin to soften it for a parka, and a boy of two years was running around getting into everything.

I looked around. The cabin had two rooms, not as dirty as some. The walls were covered with newspapers obtained from the traders at Saint Michael years ago. Everywhere around the rooms were boxes. Some were filled with dried fish, others with dried skins. Still other skins were drying on the ceiling.

I sat on a stool a few inches off the floor. The men sat on the floor talking Eskimo and laughing. Agnes Kirt, one of my students, who had married and lived at Pikmiktatik came to visit me. We talked about all her friends at Chaneliak and what we were doing in school. She told me she and her husband Johnny were happy and she had gone hunting with him many times. Now they would go up the Yukon to fish camp for the summer.

By this time, the old lady was preparing the evening meal. There was a table two inches off the floor. The men and I sat on the floor around the table. The old lady put the pot of boiled reindeer meat in the middle of the table with a small bucket of seal oil. We all took out our pocket knives. There were no dishes or utensils. I took the first piece of meat; then the men helped themselves. We cut the meat off the bones and ate with our fingers. The men dipped their meat in the seal oil but I skipped that. Of course the seal oil was dripping all over the table.

After the meat course came more tea and bread. Eskimo bread was made with white flour bought from the trader and with water. It was shaped into a flat round cake and baked. The women and children ate after we had finished. The men retired to the other room to visit and tell their Eskimo tales. Rusty and I took a walk among the willows. Ptarmigan startled us by flying out of the bushes. Their feathers were turning dark for the summer. The setting sun was red on the horizon and the fading blue sky and rosy clouds were reflected by the snow. Rusty didn't know what to make of the entire affair but I was experiencing a new culture. We returned to the cabin after passing about fifty dogs howling, barking, and trying to break their chains to fight Rusty.

In the cabin Old Man Lupon was still telling stories to his visitors. Soon Agnes and the other visitors left. Everyone knelt and said prayers. Taking my boots off, I bedded down in my sleeping bag on the only spring cot. The men put their sleeping bags on the floor. We were packed in that room like sardines. During the night the men were driving dog teams, talking a blue streak dreaming their dreams, so that it was impossible for me to sleep.

Tea and bread constituted breakfast. As soon as the dogs were harnessed, we were off. It was six-twenty in the morning. The sun was warm, the sky blue. The dogs were happy to be trotting along in the sunlight. Many sand cranes were nesting near the trail. By this time my new experiences had caught up with me and I had a terrible headache.

We reached Saint Michael about 10:00 a.m. Again the weather had changed and it was snowing when we arrived at Nell's. I was grateful to have a warm place to stay. I stayed with Nell and Herb Johnson for two days during which time the teachers from Stebbins came over to Nell's to visit and have breakfast. They had saved three thousand dollars in three years and were leaving for the States in July. They didn't enjoy Alaska. I wished we could have saved that much.

The weather cleared, and on the eighth, Jack picked me up in the mail plane and flew me to Unalakleet. I stayed at the trading post with Henry and Gladys Trager until the thirteenth. While at Unalakleet, I visited the school to observe. There were three teachers. I was able to get many supplies I needed for summer school as well as attend the birthday party of one of the teachers. One of the native teachers washed and set my hair. What a luxury! I hadn't had that much attention for over two years.

While Gladys was working at the trading post, we talked ourselves hoarse. I bought two mastodon ivory bracelets there, one black and one greenish in color. Large mastodon tusks work their way out of the Unalakleet river in the spring after the break-up. Before the white man arrived pieces of walrus and mastodon tusks were made into masks, charms, handles for drums, spear points, knives, harpoons, net weights, and seal throat plugs with carved faces. When the seal was killed, lungs were deflated and a plug was inserted into the wind pipe, so that the seal could more easily be towed behind the kayak. Later the plugs served as good luck charms. Ivory was made into combs, snow goggles, terrets for dog harnesses, miniature birds and animals. Whole walrus tusks were engraved with hunting and fishing scenes. Some of these old carvings go back as far as 780 B.C. Radio carbon dating has established the presence of humans in Alaska twenty-eight thousand years ago, though some authorities favor even an earlier date. (from *Eskimo Art*, by Cottie Burland, 1973. Published by Hamlyn, London.)

Besides the mastodon bracelets, I treasure two old pieces of walrus ivory. One is a story knife carved with a design, eight inches long and one inch wide with a hole at the top for a leather strap to hang around the neck. The other piece must have been a charm: even my Eskimos were not sure. It is a figurine five inches tall and looks like a small doll. It has a hole drilled all the way through the middle and a small hole drilled at the top for a leather thong or chain. Both pieces are dark brown from being buried in the earth for many years. These pieces were dug up at reindeer camp on Pastol Bay off Norton Sound and given to me by Joe Uisuk at Kotlik Trading Post.

Eskimos first made only practical objects of ivory but often of great beauty. After the white man and the whalers arrived, Eskimos learned to make cribbage boards and other ivory objects for sale. Ivory carving was by no means general among the Eskimos. When we were in Alaska, islanders and Seward Peninsula people were the ivory artists. Those living on Saint Lawrence Island were famous for their lattice work. Residents of King Island and Cape Prince of Wales carved well and some were successful etchers. From Nelson Island I have seen whole tusks carved with animals, birds, fish, and figurines. The Islanders came to Nome in the summer and lived in tents on the outskirts of the town to sell their wares.

A few raw (or white) walrus pieces that I have kept are a cribbage board with two carved walrus; a carved bear and a whale; two etched seals and an etched walrus, earrings decorated with etched reindeer. Many pieces I sent to relatives and friends in the States.

Old brown ivory is rare. Sometimes the seller will boil the ivory piece in dark tea to make it look old and sell it for a greater price. One summer when Perce was in Nome at the Polar Bar, a sailor had a piece of brown ivory carved in the shape of a bear. He wanted to sell it and was asking five times what its worth would be if it was white new ivory.

Perce said "Let me see it." Taking his pocket knife he scratched the bottom of the figure. It was white and had been boiled in tea. The man was very angry and wanted to fight Perce, but Perce only laughed and said, "You know you are wrong. Don't be so dishonest." Perce was with two fellow workmen; so the sailor thought better of it and left the bar with the figurine.

On May thirteenth, Jack picked me up at Unalakleet by plane. He had his five-year-old daugther with him. She kept pushing all the instruments and Jack kept pushing them back in place—a bit nerve-racking—but we landed safely at Nome. Perce was at the airport to meet us and I was happy to see him. Living alone in an isolated Eskimo village in Alaska was no fun.

While Perce was working in Nome, he lived in the bunkhouse at the mine; but while I was there we stayed with Jack's brother, Bill, and his wife, Marge. Perce worked the night shift from twelve midnight until eight in the morning, so he was able to show me the sights and introduce me to his friends. We ate, drank, and danced at the Polar Bar. A huge piece of ham with eggs, fried potatoes, toast, and coffee cost only two dollars and fifty cents! Those days are gone forever.

Carl Anderson worked with Perce. His wife, Betty, invited us to their house many mornings for Swedish hot cakes. Her aunt, Mrs. Lincoln, owned and ran the Lincoln Hotel. She was a large, friendly Finnish woman with blonde hair and bright blue eyes. She always had a boilermaker or a beer for you if you wanted it. Her long living room with many windows facing the Bering Sea was like a museum.

Old sofas, settees and an organ filled the room; portraits of her husband's family and hers hung on the walls. Her husband had been a senator for the territory of Alaska in the gold rush days. In that room, I felt as if I had stepped back into the eighteen hundreds.

One day Perce took me out to the gold dredge. It was huge. There were four hoppers. The buckets picked up the rocks and gravel, then up the ladder they went, dumping their load into the hoppers where the rocks were separated by size and the gravel and heavy gold were allowed to drop through into a box. When I looked into the box I could see many large nuggets and small pieces of gold. The gold was then separated from the gravel and taken to the Nome Bank to be melted into ingots.

I wanted to see the ingots made. That opportunity came when I met Gertrude Eaton, a hair dresser and a delightful person. Immediately we became friends. The banker was her friend. One evening Gertrude and I were invited by the banker to have cocktails and dinner at his place. He lived in a flat above the bank facing the Bering Sea with a glorious view of the sea and the ships as they lay anchored. Being a bachelor, he had a Philippino servant, who cooked and attended to all his needs. After an elegant dinner the banker took us to the basement where the gold was melted down into ingots. I had never seen so much gold: it was stacked like cord wood. In the summer these ingots, worth millions of dollars, would be shipped to the states.

Another interesting and generous person in Nome was May. She owned a small bar and had a team of thirteen white matched Siberian huskies. At Christmas she would load up her sled many times and take food, clothing and presents to people in Nome who were not as fortunate as she had been.

Then there was Mr. Polet, the storekeeper, who had been in Nome for many years—a person interested in the welfare of the people and the town.

The store sold everything: food, clothes, hardware, furniture, and art objects. Perce saw a small black basket woven of whale bone or baleen. Baleen is an elastic, horny substance growing in place of teeth in the upper jaw of certain whales, forming a series of thin parallel plates which act as a strainer. This substance is woven by the men of Point Hope into beautiful little baskets. Some of the baleen is left whole, to serve as the warp; some is split into thin strips to serve as the woof. A small piece of ivory an inch more or less in diameter is drilled with tiny holes around the edge to start the bottom of the basket. The thin strips go in the holes and weave around and around coils of baleen until the basket is the desired size. A lid is made in the same manner, weaving the split baleen over and over the coils until at the top another piece of ivory for a handle is carved, usually in the shape of an animal, on a small round base with holes drilled around the edge. This is secured by weaving the strips in and out around the handle to complete the lid of the basket. Small pieces of shaved ivory are sometimes woven over parts of the baleen to make a design. Perce bought a baleen basket at Polet's store for me and it is still one of my prized possessions.

After a month in Nome my visit was coming to a close: I had to find a way back to Saint Michael and Chaneliak. Recent weather had been too severe for Jack to fly the mail plane, but Pete Paulson was on his way to Saint Michael with supplies on his boat, the *Trader*, so I would go with him. (Miss Carlson had changed her mind about meeting me at Hamilton. She would come to Chaneliak and from there we would travel to Kwiguk with Alex on the *Daisy*.)

The icebergs were still floating offshore in the Bering Sea at Nome on June nineteenth when Pete brought his dory to the dock and rowed me and my luggage to the *Trader*. It was a small two-masted sailing ship, fifty-feet long, with a small cabin. There were no accommodations, so you carried a coffee can. You know what for! You were just one of the boys.

We had traveled a couple of hours across Norton Sound toward Saint Michael when one of the engines stopped. Pete came up to the cabin and said, "Mrs. Starritt, I want you to take over the wheel. My deck hand and I are both needed to get the engine going again. I will show you how to navigate."

"But what about the icebergs?" I asked.

"Oh just go around them. They are not too large," said

Pete. So he showed me how to read the instruments, told me what instrument numbers to stay on, taught me how to steer, and down he went to the engine room. You can't imagine how I felt out in the middle of Norton Sound with the responsibility of navigating the boat. Fortunately I saw only one iceberg and I didn't hit it. I went around it as Pete had directed. The sea was calm and the sun was high in the sky. I could see no more danger. After three hours they got the engine going again and happily I was relieved of my duty without a mishap.

We arrived at Saint Michael in the evening. I could see the *Ensee* at anchor, so Pete rowed me over to it and I got aboard. Some of the supplies that I needed for summer school were on the *Ensee*. We left at 3:45 a.m. for the Yukon and arrived at Chaneliak about 1:30 p.m. After three days at sea I was glad to be back and able to get cleaned up.

Father and the natives were still at Chaneliak when I arrived on June twenty-first. Father came to school and we began filling the medicine boxes for the natives to take to their fish camps, where they would live in tents until September, catching salmon and drying them for the coming winter. By June twenty-third everyone had left Chaneliak except the Okitkuns and me. On June twenty-eight, the *Daisy*, with Alex at the wheel, came chugging into the slew at high tide with Miss Alma Carlson on board. I was all packed and so was Alex's family. Early the next morning we took off on the *Daisy* for Kwiguk and Saltery.

Most of our natives were camped at Bill Moore's slew. We stopped to unload Alex's family and supplies. Alma examined several people who had colds, and gave them medicine. We traveled upriver and made a quick stop at Hamilton to take on some supplies for Axel Johnson who managed the Northern Commercial Trading Post at Kwiguk for George Butler.

Alma and I were both eager for our new adventures and were looking forward to teaching and caring for the children and families living on the south mouth of the Yukon River.

After arriving at Kwiguk we made arrangements to use a little church building for school. Axel loaned us two small tents, one for Alma to use for examinations and health classes and the other for living quarters at Kwiguk until our tents arrived. On the last day of June we put them up next to the church. We left the next morning on the *Argonaut* to spend a month at Saltery until the families now there moved back to Kwiguk.

Saltery was what is now called Alakanuk at the mouth of Kwikluak Pass. It was a camp owned by Northern Commercial Company, where the natives from Kwiguk fished only for king salmon for the company. The salmon were filleted, salted and put in tierces holding five hundred pounds. After the tierces were filled they were placed in a cave and covered with wet moss to keep them cool before being transported on a barge to the refrigerated boat docked at Saint Michael for shipment to New York. There the fish were smoked-dried and sold to Jewish merchants to be made into gefilte fish.

There were two permanent sheds at Saltery where the fish were filleted: one large tent for school and meetings and two small tents, one for Alma to use for an examination room, the other for our sleeping quarters. The natives' tents were scattered along the bank of the river.

On July third we started teaching. Some evenings, we had lessons for men and women, generally in separate groups, but sometimes together. On other nights we had games and sing-alongs.

It so happened, on the evening of July Fourth, we were having a celebration for everyone. The traders had given us fireworks and there were songs and native dancing. When the festivities were about finished a man from across Kwikluak Pass came into the tent and said, "Two people are dead and others dying from food poisoning. Would you come and help?"

Alma, Herb Lawrence, his sister, and I left at once in Herb's little boat, the *Reindeer*.

We docked the boat and were led to a tent, where we saw a dead man sitting up with his legs bound in a sitting position. His eyes were closed as if he were sleeping, but I had the feeling he might open his eyes any minute and ask me what I was doing in his tent. The other dead person was a young girl. Her legs were also bound into a sitting position, but she was lying on her back on a reindeer skin next to the man, who, we found out later, was her father. Two old Eskimo women were squatting next to them as if carrying on a conversation. Herb questioned the women in Eskimo and they told him the two who had died had eaten an old pike they had placed in the ground to ripen and, after digging it up, had carried it around in a five gallon gas can for a month. They had had convulsions, passing a green fluid. When the convulsions had stopped they could not move their legs. They said others had eaten the pike, including a young boy.

Herb's sister, Elizabeth, immediately gathered up the little boy and three others who had eaten the pike. We heated water on the camp fire and gave them enemas. They did pass some green fluid and also the longest tape worms I had ever seen. They were given an emetic so that they would vomit any remaining food that might be poisonous. They were ill but survived.

In fishing season, many natives bury fish heads and other fish and meat to have it ripen in the frozen tundra. There is very little acid in their diet except berries and this seems to take the place of citrus fruits and other acids.

We stayed to help with the burial. When we returned to the tent where the two corpses were, the relatives were wailing a loud, mournful chant of sorrow. The girl was being wrapped in a reindeer skin and the father in a blanket. The back of the tent was lifted and the bodies were pushed out onto the tundra. The men picked up the bodies.

Alma, Elizabeth, and I helped the two old ladies gather the girl's belongings: a wooden dish, a tin cup, clothing, a rabbit fur parka, a grass sleeping mat, sewing material, a goose down blanket, two pairs of mukluks, and a few miscellaneous articles like a comb, mittens, belt, and an old rag doll. We crawled out the back of the tent carrying her worldly possessions and walked behind the relatives and friends, who were carrying the father's personal possessions, his boat, and food for the dead to eat.

The sun was high in the sky, white clouds were floating around in the blue, the wind was blowing, and there was a chill in the air. Five times, we stopped and stood silently before we arrived at our destination. When we reached the burial place, reindeer skins were placed on the ground and the two bodies were put in a sitting position on the skins with their personal belongings. Another mournful chant was sung and we all walked silently back to camp.

The five stops represented the five days before the dead would get up and walk away. The reason they were tied in a sitting position was so that they could easily rise and walk to another world. No knives, axes, or anything else with a sharp edge could be used for five days by living relatives. There was also a taboo that no living relative could hunt for a month.

I thought to myself, it was best for them to die in the summer because fishing would not be taboo. Because relatives could not use anything with a sharp edge, friends in the camp would cut their wood and help them. After five days the bodies would be placed in two wooden boxes supported by two uprights about five feet above the tundra. Wooden headboards with carved masks of human faces were sometimes placed near the burial boxes in this part of the tundra, south of the Yukon River.

It was depressing there on the large desolate waste of the tundra; and it really wasn't pleasant to see a dead man sitting in a tent as if his eyes would open any second. We were glad to return to Saltery.

The people living on the tundra near Black River still partially believed in Shamanistic practices. This part of Alaska had been touched very little by the white man.

Before the white man's invasion of Alaska, Eskimos had a different concept of a supreme deity. Their religion included respect for the spirit of all beings. All possessed a spiritual power. And they followed shaman practices. Every person, animal, fish, and bird had a shade, a patron, who protected him. The universe was filled with spiritual power.

The following are quotes from *Alaska Natives* by Dewey Anderson, Ph.D., Assistant in Educational Research, Stanford University, and Walter Crosby Eells, Ph.D., Professor of Education, Stanford University:

"According to Dr. E.W. Nelson, who lived among the Eskimos at Saint Michael from 1877 to 1881, the Eskimos conceived of two parts to the other world to which departed shades of animals and humans went. The upper world was the abode of the shades of the shamans and those who died through accident or starvation. It was the reward world, located somewhere in the sky, where these fortunate shades lived in plenty.

"The shades of people departed this life from natural causes went to an underworld where there were also villages of animal shades. These shades were entirely dependent upon their earthly relatives for material comfort. A supply of food and water and certain essential personal belongings were placed on the grave to be used by the departed shade journeying to the other world. Also, at the feast of the dead in the *Khashggi* the shade was invited by his relatives and friends to come and partake of the offerings made there. The shade was supposed actually to enter in the person of the child to whom his name had been given and to be fed and reclothed in the gifts bestowed upon the namesake.

"Thieves and evil persons were to be uncomfortable after death, and even were believed to return to haunt the vicinity of their burial places."

Alma and I continued our work at Saltery. Alma was examining everyone, finding much tuberculosis, especially in the babies and children. This was caused by the mother chewing the food and putting it into the infant's mouth. We were giving all the babies and children cod liver oil every day and keeping records which I was to continue the following summer when Alma would not be with me.

For recreation at night, Elizabeth, Herb, one of the natives, and I went belgua hunting in two dories with outboard motors. The first night, we saw nothing. Leo Andrews and I were in one dory and Elizabeth and Herb in the other. The second night Leo shot a *beluga*, but before Herb could throw the spear with the float, the whale sank. On the third night, when the whale came up to breathe, Herb shot it and Leo threw the spear into the *beluga* with the rope tied to it. We fastened the rope to the boat and towed the whale to shore, where it was cut up and divided. The *beluga* was small, about two hundred pounds, but the oil and meat were very important to the natives. Leo got my share since I hadn't gone native and learned to eat whale meat.

Our stay at Saltery was coming to a close. The king salmon run was over, the fish were packed in tierces and placed on the two barges. The last day of school I taught in the morning. We had been at Saltery nineteen days.

The wind was blowing a gale when the *Ensee* and the *Argonaut* arrived to tow the barges to Saint Michael. The camp was breaking up. All the families were moving. In only an hour all our supplies and tents were on the *Ensee* and we were dead tired. Captain Holsher sent us to his cabin to sleep while traveling to Kwiguk, where we arived at 4:00 a.m. We continued our sleeping at the Northern Commercial Trading Post in Axel's quarters. He woke us at noon to tell us our tents were up and ready, next to the church.

We walked down the riverbank past the huge barn where the Northern Commercial Company smoked strips of silver salmon and past Pete Jorgensen's tall smoke house where he was drying sides of king salmon, a process which took six weeks. His two older children were sitting on the boardwalk in front of their house taking care of their little brother. When we reached our quarters we started getting ready to open school by unpacking our meager supplies. At midnight we decided to stop and let the children help us in the morning.

Twenty-one children of all ages from five to fifteen arrived the next day. Alma took the girls into her tent to teach health habits and sewing. I took the boys into the church. There were a few benches but most sat on the floor. We started labeling everything: windows, benches, doors, pictures; we printed our names and labeled our clothing. We drew pictures of ourselves and hung them around the room.

The next day we started writing little readers with illustrations about Kwiguk and how the people lived. The boys also read little books my other Eskimo students had written about livng on the Yukon River. Since these children had never gone to school, we were all having great fun. The second day Alma took the boys for their health lessons. After the first two days, I had all the children for school and play, while Alma made home calls, examined the adults, treated the sick, and sometimes took the older girls to teach them baby care, sewing, and vocabulary.

Every night we had meetings and classes. The first night everyone arrived, children and all. We told them our plans and asked for their help. We needed tables or anything that could be used as desks as well as play equipment. The fathers and older boys turned out to be very inventive. Some made desks with seats out of wooden boxes that had held two five-gallon cans of gas. Others made benches and tables to fit the small children. Eric and Morris, two of the older boys, arrived with tables and benches made from old boards they had found lying around the village. Paul Redfox made a blackboard; Charlie Redfox and Jimmy Boy made jump ropes and fashioned two kickballs of sealskin stuffed with reindeer hair. Anthony made basketball goals with the help of Paul and Charlie. Pete Jorgensen had told Alma to come to the house as they had extra things they didn't use; Mrs. Jorgensen had made grass mats for the floor of Alma's tent; so we had a collection of usable household items. our seating problem was solved, and we would store the equipment at the trading post for the next summer.

Every night many children would come to play basketball while we had classes for the men and women. After meetings everyone would play games or watch until eleven o'clock.

After Pete had finished smoking one two-hundred-pound batch of king salmon, he went to Hamilton to ship it to the States. When he returned, he told me Perce had come back from Nome for a few days. He and George Butler would come to Kwiguk on the *Mildred.*

Alma and I had been teaching ten days when they arrived towing George's powerful outboard and the *Argonaut.* The *Mildred* and the *Argonaut* were freighting supplies to Black River Trading Post; Alma and I would go with them to give care to the natives in the fish camps along the way.

Meanwhile George was checking the books and restocking the Kwiguk Trading Post with Perce's help. They wanted to visit Pat Murphy, the postmaster, who was married to a five-foot-tall Eskimo woman named Annie.

Annie made excellent home brew and liked to drink it. She could take a large tin cup full of beer, make one fast turn around, and the beer would be gone. George and Perce, after their business was completed, went in the outboard to Pat's and tied up at his little floating dock.

As I have told you before, George was a joker and a talker, and the beer was the main reason he and Perce went to visit Pat and Annie. They were hoping Annie would offer them enough beer to take back to Hamilton. As it happened, she only offered them one drink, but she kept looking at George's green rain slicker. Finally George said, "Annie, would you like to have my slicker?"

That was all she was waiting for. George took off his slicker; Annie put it on. It reached to the floor on her but little did she care, she was all smiles. Then the drinks came in plenty until Perce and George were feeling a bit high and it was time to leave.

They jumped into the boat, forgetting to untie it, and off they dashed up the river with the little dock trailing behind them. Annie yelled and jumped up and down on the shore in her green slicker. Pat yelled and waved. Finally, those two with a little too much beer looked around to see why Annie and Pat were making such a fuss and discovered their haul. They made one big wide turn and returned it.

Annie and Pat weren't too happy, but when Perce and George helped to secure the dock to shore, Annie was smiling again. There were many handshakes before Perce and George went on their way.

Perce stayed a few days with George at Hamilton. During this time, the native Russian Orthodox priest arrived alone in his little boat to visit the few natives who still believed in the Orthodox religion.

He always took a bottle of wine as a gift to George in appreciation for the use of his dock. But George was up to his usual tricks. He told Perce to slip five dollars to the priest for the bottle, which Perce did.

Then George took the priest aside where Perce couldn't hear what he was saying. George said to the priest, "That fellow who gave you the five dollars is a Deputy Marshal. He will probably arrest you for selling the wine, but if you give me seventeen bottles I will convince him to let you go on down the river to Saint Michael."

The frightened little priest gave George the wine. George

was always up to some mischief. Probably this was one reason he could endure the isolation of the north for many years while he worked for the Northern Commercial Company. After this prank Perce returned to Nome on the mail plane and finished the season at the mine.

On August third, Alma and I left Kwiguk on the *Mildred* towing a small boat, the *Argonaut,* for side trips. We stopped at Saltery, where Elizabeth and Herb came aboard with their supplies. We left Saltery around 6:00 p.m. for the Bering Sea. Just before we reached the sea, the *Mildred* anchored for the night. Herb, the deckhands and I got into the *Argonaut* and went along the shore of the river for wood Herb needed for the winter at the Black River Trading Post.

The next morning we entered the rough sea. The *Mildred* was bouncing up and down. I was glad I was a good sailor. The *Argonaut* was being tossed from side to side. I thought we were going to lose her but thanks to Alex Kazenkoff, who was pilot on the *Mildred,* we finally reached the fish camp at the mouth of Black River and tied up. We unloaded the few personal things we needed and the medical supplies; the deckhands put up our tent and the *Mildred* went on its way up Black River to the Trading Post. While the *Mildred* went upriver to unload, we stayed three days at the fish camp taking census, examining each adult and child, and giving out medicines and advice.

There were forty families along the riverbank, as many as seven or eight in a tent. As we came to each tent, I couldn't believe my eyes. In front of each tent were piles of ducklings and goslings too small to fly that had been clubbed to death. Alma told me that the natives in this part of Alaska had a drive, herding the nesting birds into a large group and clubbing them. As many as a thousand birds would be killed at one time and divided among all in the village. Due to the lack of reindeer skins, the natives needed the down for parkas and bedding. Since there were few regulations and little contact with whites, these natives were living much as their ancestors had lived.

Herb also told me a white woman was a curiosity. George's wife, Louise, was the only white woman many of the natives had seen until Alma and I arrived.

As we made our rounds, I took the census and Alma

did the examining. As usual we found a great deal of tuberculosis. In one tent as Alma was examining a woman's mouth and throat, she found a large growth. I had never seen anything like it. It resembled a sponge inside the right side of her mouth. When we left the tent I asked Alma about it. She said, "It's a cancer. The woman has only a few weeks to live." It was a horrible looking thing but by this time, I was getting used to seeing unusual sights.

The *Mildred* returned on the morning of August sixth. We packed and got aboard. Then the natives came aboard and Alma pulled teeth for a day and a half.

When the *Mildred* tried to move, it was stuck in the mud and we had to wait for high tide. We finally got underway, but near Saltery a blow came up and the *Argonaut* got a rope tangled in her running gear; so we tied up to the bank to untangle the rope. We finally reached Kwiguk at 1:30 p.m. the tenth of August. As we docked the children were all on the bank waiting for us, so I held school for two hours. I wondered where they all came from; there were at least thirty.

Alma stayed only a week more at Kwiguk, then left for Mountain Village. I stayed until September first, teaching and canning dried salmon strips in oil to send to relatives and friends in the States. Then Andrew Prince came after me in our dory, the *Loon*.

We left Kwiguk late at night. We arrived at Hamilton at two in the morning, I threw my sleeping bag on the store counter and slept there the rest of the night. George never locked the store door. Nobody stole in that part of the country: there was no place to run and hide. Next morning I went up to George's house, had breakfast, took a much-needed bath, made out bills to be sent to the Juneau office, bought a new radio for one hundred and seventeen dollars and a windcharger, which George had previously ordered for us, to provide lights at Chaneliak.

Rain was coming down in bucketfuls so George loaned me a rain outfit. Andrew and I loaded the *Loon* and we were on our way home to Chaneliak. Just above Kotlik, we saw a luftack. Andrew chased it for an hour, then I took over the kicker so that he could throw the spear. Making too sharp a turn with the boat, I almost threw Andrew into the river with the seal! Andrew thought it best we give up the chase; I was thinking "I'm not too skilled at this game," so we headed home. When I arrived, Perce had returned from Nome. He and Chiklik were painting the inside of the classroom, putting a new floor upstairs in the storeroom, and building a new storm shed off the kitchen with a small bathroom, where we put the chemical toilet. Perce installed my new oil cookstove in the kitchen. It was such a comfort not to have to build a wood fire or use that terrible Alaskan coal, which I was more than happy to give to our natives in the village. I had only to turn the switch and the blaze burned brightly.

My older girls were overjoyed with the cookstove for their bread, cake and cookie baking when we had our entertainments. They used the new stove to bake cookies for the Halloween party, where everyone had great fun.

The married men ate apples from a string, the unmarried men and boys bobbed for apples in a tub of water. What a mess! There was one unfortunate happening. Simon Andrews had just returned from Hamilton where he had contracted the measles germ and spread it around at the party.

The weather continued to be below freezing all of October. This was the most severe winter anyone had seen in many years. Everyone was waiting for high tide to get their boats out of the water, but that never happened. Fortunately, Andrew and Perce had taken our boat, the *Loon,* out of the water when we had returned from Kwiguk. The *Daisy* looked very strange sitting in the ice with all the other smaller boats frozen in the slew. Alex, Perce, and all the other men in the village helped to saw them out of the ice.

Because of the early freeze-up, there were many unexpected happenings. Warren Fergensen and Varnell went through the ice at Kotzebue in Varnell's truck. Fergensen was drowned but Varnell, Perce's friend with whom he had worked at Nome that summer, was saved.

The *Ensee* had gone upriver the first part of October. We were wondering if she would return. She came back in the middle of October, but froze in the Yukon about a mile from Chaneliak. Captain Holsher, Captain Olsen and Stewart, the engineer, were living on the *Ensee* and very uncomfortable; so I invited them to stay with us until it was safe for the plane to land and they could return to the States. Captain Holsher was a southerner and liked baking powder biscuits with gravy. I made biscuits and gravy every day for three weeks.

At night we played penny ante and listened to the radio. The news was very bleak. Hitler was marching through Europe and bombing England. It was frightening. The plane arrived on November seventh and flew the three men to Anchorage. They would return in the Spring.

On November eighth the first mail and freight planes began flying over every few days, hauling freight to Mountain Village. We had been very fortunate: our school and personal freight had been delivered by the *Mildred* in August. Father however, didn't receive his freight; so we were lending him food and other supplies.

Frank Williams and Herb Johnson were hauling freight by dog team, an expensive way to get their supplies and Father's to the store in Chaneliak. The freighter *Boxer*, didn't arrive at Saint Michael until the twelfth of October. Herb and Frank had a difficult time unloading because of the shell ice. When the *Boxer* anchored off Unalakleet in Norton Sound, Henry Trager had to break ice to get his boat, the *Tex*, out to lighter the freighter. He had almost reached the *Boxer* when a north wind came up and blew so hard that he couldn't reach the freighter; so Captain Bush pulled out for Seattle, afraid of an ice jam. Henry had to break ice all the way back to Unalakleet. This situation left his trading post short of supplies for the winter.

The cold weather continued: on November nineteenth it was twenty below zero. That was like seventy below in Fairbanks because of the humidity.

On a beautiful clear day, I looked toward the *Ensee*, frozen in the white ice, and I would have sworn that it was on fire the way the sun was shining on it's orange-red smokestack. I was almost ready to alert the men in the village and send them to the *Ensee* to put out the fire when I decided it was only a reflection of the bright sun.

The cold weather didn't help our measles outbreak either. Every family in our village and the surrounding villages had someone sick with the measles. I had to close school for two weeks. Perce and I spent ten hours a day doctoring and seeing that everyone stayed in bed. As a result, we did not have any deaths.

Old Stephan Kameroff told us that in 1900 there had been a measles epidemic and people had died by the hundreds. Because of the fever they would run out and jump in the rivers and slews. There were so many deaths that the Army from the base at Saint Michael came to bury them. They found people dead sitting in the doorways of their cabins and tents. Bodies were everywhere on the tundra near the villages. They dug large ditches and threw the bodies from each village together. You could still see where there had been several large villages. As a result there were very few old people in the villages around Chaneliak.

Carlson arrived two weeks before Christmas. Our measles epidemic was over. She visited the families, had several meetings, and made house calls.

Father was at Chaneliak for Christmas and had his usual large celebrations, Mass every day, and services in the evening. Alma and I attended Midnight Mass on Christmas. Due to church activities, I had a short Christmas program.

After Christmas, Alma and I went to Hamilton. I had to see George about summer school plans and make house calls with Alma. I was learning new health techniques every day. I had become what you would call a traveling nurse, assistant, advisor, teacher, and jack of all trades for the natives of the lower Yukon River country.

Alma had lost some of her interest in our section of the country. She was more concerned with Hooper Bay. She said it was a native's paradise with an abundance of clams, ducks, geese, and hair seals by the thousands.

We were staying with George on New Year's Eve. We worked on reports and played Chinese checkers for entertainment. On New Year's Day a plane landed at Hamilton to take Alma to Hooper Bay.

I was going home and had bought a writing desk from George that had been his wife's. Old Appa, or Charley Prince, didn't think much of putting it on the sled but little did I care. He had been paid very well. Alma had given him ten dollars to take us to Hamilton and I was giving him ten more to take me back to Chaneliak.

On our way home, the reindeer committee plane with Sam Kendrick swooped down close over our dog team to say hello—a little too close for comfort—I thought they were going to land on us but up they went on their way. When I returned home Father had gone to Stebbins. The natives wanted to use the schoolhouse for dancing: so they brought their drums over and danced for three nights celebrating the New Year. All three nights the girls and I served tea and cookies. The girls were using my new cookstove to bake the cookies and enjoying every minute of it.

Since Father was gone, we had Eskimo dancing and games every Sunday night, plus adult English classes every Wednesday night for the men and Thursday night for the women. Mamie was my interpreter and helper. The people spoke only Eskimo at home, but they were anxious to speak and write English; so all the adults in the village attended. On April first, Father arrived with Bishop Fitzgerald and my evening activities stopped.

We were very impressed with the Bishop. I invited him and Father to dinner. Once he sneaked away from Father and came in our back door where Perce was working in the kitchen. He and Perce had a hot toddy and a long visit. He was doing a little checking into the activities of Father and the natives and also to see what we were doing for the Eskimos. He stayed a week in Chaneliak, then a plane arrived with the *Ensee* men and the Bishop returned to Fairbanks. Father took a dog team to Stebbins.

The *Ensee* men returned bearing gifts, including celery which we hadn't tasted for months. Stewart, the engineer, brought me a camera, which I had trouble learning to adjust. I ruined the first roll of film, snapping the *Ensee* in the ice. I really wanted those pictures.

There were other gifts too numerous to mention. The men stayed a week with us while they cleaned the *Ensee* to get it livable. After they moved back to the *Ensee,* we would walk across the tundra almost every night to play penny ante with the crew; sometimes the captain would join us.

The slew still had some broken ice. It was unsafe even for a small dory to travel on the slew or river, but the ice was breaking up fast.

Thomas O'Macky, the cook, Dummy, as he was called because he could not speak, was one excellent poker player. How he could bluff! The expression on his face was a complete blank so you never knew if he had a good or poor hand. He ended up with most of the pennies. We were told he had been black-listed by most of the soldiers at the fort in the early days because he was too lucky and won their paychecks. I could believe it! He had cooked at Fort Saint Michael in the gold rush days on the Yukon, and stayed after the fort was discontinued, working as a cook on the *Ensee* for the Northern Commercial Company. When we played cards Dummy always fed us at midnight before we started back home. One night he put canned milk over sardines and baked them in the oven for our treat! How good it tasted, before we trudged back to the school over the frozen mossy tundra.

On Easter Sunday, the Wilsons, native Lutheran missionaries, and their daughter arrived from Mountain Village on their way to the Unalakleet Mission. They had sent us vegetables every fall and had entertained us in their home at Unalakleet; so I had asked them to stay with us when traveling between their two missions. The Lutheran missionaries encouraged many of the Eskimo dances, customs and legends, while other missionaries repressed the Eskimo ways. When our natives found out they were staying a few days, they wanted to have their dances. We were happy to have them entertain the Wilsons. In the evenings they brought over their three drums and the songs and dances began.

Reverend Wilson told me more than I had ever known about the dances. They had been taught from one generation to the next. Some might be hundreds of years old. While our natives were dancing he told me the stories.

One male dancer had been butted by the horns of a reindeer on a hunt. One woman went on the ice to fish for pike. Then one old woman was tired: she had picked cranberries all day on the cold windy tundra and wanted to sleep. Then the younger girls were called up to dance the same dances. Four men called the young men out on the floor so that they could learn the reindeer dance from their fathers. In one comical dance old Waska put on a mask and sat in the middle of the floor. Three women stood behind him trying to mimic everything he did while making fun of him. Waska was throwing his arms around, patting his head, kicking his feet out from under him as in a Russian dance. The audience was hilarious, with everyone clapping hands to the rhythm of the drums.

All the dancers were wearing white cotton gloves to make their hands more conspicuous. This was an old custom. Skin gloves made of mink, muskrat, or Arctic hare were worn or carried at the khashgii festivals before the traders came, but now it was easier to buy white canvas gloves.

These were enjoyable evenings for us and the entire village. My school children had made crepe paper flowers as Easter gifts for the Wilsons. The Wilsons were more than grateful for their flowers and their stay with us. Early one morning, after many handshakes from the natives and from us, they left by dog team for Unalakleet.

The last day of April, I closed school. I had been teaching every Saturday all year and had a total of one hundred and seventy-six days. Many reports had to be completed and sent to the Juneau office. Packing and cleaning were to be done and plans for summer school at Kwiguk had to be made. Perce and Chiklik were painting the outside of the building, putting shelves in the dispensary and doing other maintenance on the school building and shop so that everything would be ready in the fall when we returned. The village was almost deserted as it was muskrat season and many families were hunting.

On May fifth, Perce could walk on the ice in the slew, but by May eighth it was too dangerous. On May eleventh at 2:37 p.m. the ice went out on the Nenana River and someone won a fifty-thousand dollar pool. We knew it wouldn't be long before the ice moved out of the mouth of the Yukon and the Ensee and its crew could go about their business for the summer months.

Then on May thirteenth Dr. Stapins and his wife, a nurse, flew in with diphtheria toxoid. They told us Alma Carlson was in the Bethel Hospital very ill with diphtheria and that many were dying at Hooper Bay and Scammon Bay. The doctor gave us our shots and instructions that we were to give injections to everyone, natives and whites, who had not been immunized previously. He left the toxoid and said if we needed more to wire the Mountain Village hospital and they would send it down by plane. This didn't make us too happy..

We thought they could have stayed a couple of hours and given the shots to those left in the village, but that was our job, according to the doctor. The shots were to be given at once.

The same day, with some ice in the slew and on the river, Paul Yunak put his dory with outboard in the slew and off we went to Kotlik. Perce got off at the *Ensee* to give the shots to the crew and I went on to the village. There were only eight people there. I explained the importance of the diphtheria shots and directed them to send word to the people out hunting to come to school for their shots.

We returned home at midnight. Early the next morning we went to Pastolik. There were still fourteen in the village, all of whom received their shots. I tried to take pictures but without success: I still wasn't working the camera correctly.

We saw hundreds of snow geese that had returned to nest. Paul wanted to shoot some but they were too wild to be approached. Many of the natives had heard the news about the diphtheria. When we returned to school, we worked all day giving shots. People were coming from Hamilton and other villages miles away. We were very busy for the next few weeks.

On May eighteenth, the *Ensee* came to the point at the mouth of the slew and docked at the Northern Commercial Store. Captain Holsher, Olsen, Dummy, and Harold Steward had one of the crew row them to the school to join us for dinner, listen to the news, and play cards.

The war news was getting worse every day. Hitler was closer to Paris; Belgium was giving up; Italy had joined the Germans; Great Britain was bearing the brunt of the war; the United States had sent planes to help Britain. We were afraid now we would be drawn into the war.

About this time Mr. Hess with the Alaskan Highways Department flew into Chaneliak to look for possible sites for an airfield at or near the mouth of the Yukon. He also asked us to watch for unusual activities or strangers. We were now certain that United States was preparing for a possible invasion and that Alaska was a vital part of our defenses.

As the ice had moved out of Norton Sound, the *Mildred* left Saint Michael with freight for the lower Yukon to be transferred to the *Ensee.* The boats were to meet at reindeer camp where there were several families who hadn't received their shots; so Perce boarded the *Ensee* for reindeer camp. He would also help with the freight since some of it was for us, including materials for the summer school at Kwiguk. I stayed at Chaneliak to give shots to anyone who might come to school and to work on the primer and songs I was writing for the Kwiguk summer school.

As the rains were beginning, I had the men put out our water barrels. When Father set out his bright red barrels, the church looked like a fire house. Father furnished water to some of the old Eskimos who stayed in the village for the summer.

Water on the tundra in summer was a problem. We had several cases of concentrated lime juice to put into the drinking water. Like last season's eggs, water became rank. But the eggs were fresh now and Old Lady Theresa from Pastolik gave me two and a half dozen duck eggs, a real treat.

Perce had returned from reindeer camp and we were almost ready to move to Kwiguk.

George Butler came down from Hamilton with his new speedboat and messages from the Juneau office. He had been a true friend and a great help in starting the summer school. George told us the king salmon were starting to run; so he and his crew were leaving soon for Saltery and we would be on our way to Kwiguk with him.

On June twentieth Tom Keys was helping us move. He had borrowed Joe Usiak's boat because it was larger than ours; we would tow the *Loon* loaded with supplies. As we left Chaneliak, I was sitting on top of our baggage writing reports while Rusty, our dog, slept at my feet.

When we turned into the Yukon, a mother duck and eight ducklings were swimming swiftly along to get out of our way. After five hours on the Yukon we reached Hamilton where the Mildred was loaded and waiting for us.

We arrived at Kwiguk at 10:00 p.m. About a hundred people were lining the bank as we docked. A young boy had fallen off Alstrom's boat and drowned. They were dragging the river for his body. It was never recovered, for the river was flowing fast. The body was probably carried out to sea. In another week, Perce would return to Nome for the summer. During that week, Herb arrived from Black River. Perce and Herb decided to go to Axel Alstrom's trading post to visit and enjoy a few drinks. They had been there several hours and were feeling their beers when a plane landed on the river with two fur buyers. Axel didn't want Perce and Herb there while he was discussing fur prices.

Herb had already gone to sleep on the dock near a large canvas, covering lumber and barrels. Perce pushed Herb under the canvas, jumped in the dory and rowed back to the school. In the evening, after the fur buyers left, one of Axel's children came and asked Perce to come back to the trading post. Axel was waiting for him on the dock. "What happened to Herb?" he inquired, assuming Herb had gone with Perce. "Oh, my lord! He still must be under the canvas," answered Perce. They rushed to uncover him. The day had been warm and he was lying in a big wet imprint of himself, still asleep but alive. They threw water on him. He was revived but Perce thinks to this day that he could have killed the man. Herb thought it a joke. He lost a few pounds.

Alma arrived looking thinner and rather pale from her bout with diphtheria. She didn't seem to have much energy: she wasn't her old peppy self. Nevertheless, we promptly visited all the homes and tents to ask everyone to come to the night meetings.

Alma helped with the teaching as well as doing her health work. We had puppet plays showing baby care, first-aid, and the danger of eating rotten fish. The children read and illustrated Eskimo legends as the basis for puppet plays.

The first two days thirty-six children arrived at the school, twenty-six small ones and ten boys ranging from ten to sixteen years of age. The first two days, before the men had the tent platforms built, we laid a canvas on the ground and sat in a circle for our reading lessons out of the primers I had written about the village, the Yukon, the tundra, and what happens in the four seasons. The rest of the day we played games and sang, then walked a quarter of a mile to the store, where we talked about all the things in the store and labelled them in English.

Axel Alstrom had twin boys, ten years of age. He would send them to Eklutna Industrial School in September. They were intelligent, but their only schooling had been our summer school the previous year. I wanted desperately to have them read before they went to Eklutna, so I began to work extra time every day, giving them reading lessons. By the end of August they would be at fourth grade level and able to read parts of the newspaper. With arithmetic they had few problems since they had helped their Dad at the trading post. They were friendly boys who liked to learn and see new things; I hoped their new experiences would be happy ones.

Before Perce left for Nome, the *Ensee* arrived with our freight. We received only the lumber for the tent platforms and the one room cabin but not the tents. As Perce and I stood on the edge of the river watching the unloading and talking with Captain Holsher, the bank under me broke away and down I dropped ten feet. Captain Holsher just stood there, making motions toward the river, not saying a word, with his mouth wide open. Perce couldn't see me, then he looked over the bank and there I was on a little ledge jutting out into the river. He could see I was hurt. He jumped down on the ledge to help. If I hadn't fallen on the ledge, I would have gone into the swift, deep-flowing water where I might have drowned. But luck was with me; I only had a swollen ankle. Many Eskimo villages had been moved because of the sloughing off of the riverbank on the low tundra delta of the Yukon. I had learned my lesson; I would never get too close to the river's edge again!

Perce has always said I talk too much and don't watch where I'm stepping. My ankle was so swollen, Alma had double duty for a couple of days. I just stayed in one place and heard reading lessons and read stories to the children.

Because our tents had not arrived, Alstrom loaned me two twelve by fourteen tents; but he didn't have a fourteen by twenty tent for the school. I got the material from him and had Mrs. Redfox make a tent. If we received the tents later, Alstrom would take them in return for the ones I had borrowed. He also gave us a little tent for the children to use for tea parties and a playhouse.

Perce, Tom, and the other men cut the grass, cleaned the land, built the tent platforms and a small cabin for me, and put up the flag pole. We were ready to begin our summer at Kwiguk.

After Perce left, Alma and I worked through the month of July. On August first, Alma went to Black River, then on to Hooper Bay. During the month of August I did all the health work and teaching alone.

On August fourteenth, Richard Kozenenkoff came from Hamilton with our dory, the *Loon,* to take me to Akulurak Mission to check on the immunization shots of the people and to leave extra toxoid. I stayed one night. This was a Catholic mission supported by Bing Crosby and run by a priest, several nuns, and native brothers. There were over a hundred children. Some were boarded at the school, others lived in the village. I was escorted through the school. The girls did beautiful handwork. All the children helped with various chores, including the catching and drying of salmon.

Until the end of August I taught at Kwiguk. After we packed the tents, desks, benches and supplies in the cabin for the next summer, Richard and I started back to Chaneliak. At Hamilton, we stopped for a day to pick up mail and visit with George. When we left for Chaneliak it was calm, but as we neared Bill Moore's slew, the wind was so strong we were making no headway on the river and had to stop for several hours. Then to make things worse, the ten horsepower motor stopped and we had to use the little five horsepower motor the rest of the way home. A trip that usually lasted three hours took us eight.

Perce had already returned from Nome. Our freight was all in the school building for the coming year. Perce had installed the new oil stove in the classroom, plus windmill and generator for lights, a dispensary, new floors and fresh paint inside and out. With all the other improvements we had made in the past four years, we felt as if civilization had come to Chaneliak.

Before school opened, the older girls and I decided to take the *Loon* and go on the tundra along the riverbank to rob the mice nests of roots. By this time I was handling the dory and the outboard motor fairly well, no longer afraid I would get lost in the neighboring slews, but I still didn't venture too far from Chaneliak. Having no other vegetables, the families needed the willow and other wild roots that the mice store for winter under a layer of moss. The Eskimos would eat the roots raw or boil them with meat or fish.

Six girls and I started out about 9:00 a.m. Packing firewood and a lunch of tea, fresh water, dried salmon, raisins and bread, we were off on our root hunt. We traveled down the slew to the river and turned up the Yukon. It was cold and windy, but we were warm in our Arctic hare parkas. After traveling a couple of miles toward Kotlik the girls said we were in a good place to stop; so I beached the dory. We left our lunch and dry wood in the boat and started looking for the roots.

I went with Theresa. The other girls paired off and started walking in various directions on the tundra. Each pair of girls had brought a digging tool and a cotton sack. The tool was a forked stick or two sticks nailed together making a V at one end. There was a hook at the other end to turn the moss up and uncover the nest. Theresa and I walked among the tall grass on the tundra until we came to a rise in the moss that seemed to give under our feet. Here was the nest.

We took the tool, placed it at the end of the nest, lifted the moss and there were the roots, about three inches long, neatly piled for the winter. We placed the roots in our cloth sack. We found four more nests, filled our sack, returned to the dory, and started the fire for tea. By this time the other girls were returning with their sacks filled. After hot tea and something to eat, we all felt more comfortable.

The wind was getting stronger. There were white caps on the river. We had been gone for six hours; it was time to start home with our loot. The river was rough and we took a few sprays of water over the dory, but the girls were laughing and talking and thought it great fun. We made several more trips for roots before the river froze up in the middle of October.

Taking families in the *Loon* to gather cranberries was another autumn activity. One day Lea Aparezuk, and her four children, Joe, Theresa, Marie, and George (the first baby I had delivered, now four years old) took the dory, and up the slew we went to some low bush cranberry patches.

Joe, now fifteen, had just completed making his sled, trained his dogs and graduated. He could run the outboard and help me with the dory. We took, besides our usual lunch, sealskin buckets, coffee cans, and a wooden barrel to be filled with the berries. There were also several woven grass mats that would be used to catch the berries as we shook the bushes. It was a calm day and late in the fall; there were blessedly few mosquitoes. As we traveled up the slew, Lea and the girls were singing Eskimo songs about picking berries.

After several miles we reached a large patch of berries and stopped. Spreading the mats under the bushes we filled some of our containers, then went on and found another patch. After a few more stops, barrel, buckets and cans were filled. We made a fire and had our tea and lunch while watching the birds. The ducklings and goslings were big enough to fly and getting ready for their long trip south. The terns and swallows were darting here and there and the seagulls stalked around eyeing our food.

These were special times for all of us. Lea told old legends and related berry picking experiences. Little George had a great time running around on the tundra chasing the birds. The men seldom took their women berrying. Sometimes they would take them to the patch and leave them overnight, but this was a hardship on the women and children. It was getting cold and after a full day of berry picking we were glad to get home.

The other berry we had was the moss berry. It grew everywhere on the tundra. At recess we would pick them to eat and for the children to take home after school. They were full of seeds, less palatable than the cranberry and they did not keep through the winter.

In September Pete Paulsen sailed the *Trader* into the Yukon on his way to Pitkas Point where his partner ran the station. Pete would spend the winter there. He stopped at the mouth of the slew with our mail. We went down to pick it up and visit. Pete had a case of brandy on board; we talked him out of four bottles. We were to spend Christmas with George at Hamilton and would have a

Christmas drink, we thought.

Sam Kendrick flew in some time in November on reindeer business and one bottle disappeared. That left three, so I decided that one bottle was for Perce, one for George, and the other was mine. We went to Hamilton a week before Christmas. I gave George his bottle: it disappeared; then Perce's disappeared; but mine was intact and hidden away so that those two fellows couldn't find it. When Christmas Eve arrived, I doled it out in thimblefuls, much to their disgust; but on Christmas Day we and our guests, George's two helpers, had a snifter of brandy.

Just before they flew south the helpers had killed three snow geese and frozen them. I had never before seen so much fat on birds. The whole carcass was lined with an inch or more of fat. We had to peel it off before roasting them. No wonder they can fly such long distances when they leave the north country! George's cook and I prepared a Christmas dinner fit for a king, even if we had to use canned fruits and vegetables. A great feast was had by all on Christmas Day, 1940.

IV. Shadow of Things to Come

In the winter of 1940, two German men appeared on the frozen Yukon towing with a tractor a wanaka (house) and a boat on a large barge. The older man was short and fat and was the boss. The younger man, his nephew, was tall and had very large ears. The Eskimos thought this a queer sight and gave the young man an Eskimo name, "Big Ears."

Being a bit nervous about them, Perce and I asked them where they were going. They said they were just traveling on the lower part of the Yukon for the winter and spring to learn about the people and the fishing. The natives had seen a great deal of meteorological and radio equipment in the *wanaka*, a fact which made us suspicious since the war was getting closer to us.

Cordell Hull had called Japan's bluff: we would help China and England and support Australia and the East Indies. England was reopening the Burma Road and Hitler's troops had marched into Romania. Later, when we returned to the States in the summer of '42, we would be visited by F.B.I. men to ask what we knew of the two Germans, who were under investigation and suspected of being spies. We never learned the outcome of the investigation.

After freezeup in October I was sick in bed for two weeks with sinus and the flu, or maybe I just needed a rest.

The second week in November the first mail plane arrived with Collins, the game warden, and Rhodes, his assistant, to pick up any fur that was illegal. I had ordered ten skins of land otter from Axel Alstrom, which he was keeping for me until the next summer. I was to have a fur coat but the game warden flew into Kwiguk where he picked up some pale mink, which was illegal, as well as my otter, which happened to be legal; so I would come out of Alaska without an otter coat. Needless to say, I was disappointed.

Early one morning near the end of November, Jimmy Kamenkoff from Kotlik came after me by dog team. Mary Agnes had been in labor for three days and she couldn't deliver. We rushed to Kotlik with the maternity supplies. When we entered the cabin, there was a box in the middle of the bed. Mary Agnes was leaning over it in great pain. I had her lie down, examined her and found that the fetus was slightly turned: Alma Carlson had shown me how to turn the fetus so that the head would be in the correct position. I was frightened, thinking that I might injure or kill both Mary Agnes and the baby; but as there was no one else to help I proceeded to try. My attempt was successful. I continued to encourage her with her breathing and labor. After three hours, a baby boy was born.

The same winter that Mary Agnes gave birth, Justine, Mike's wife, was pregnant. She was a frail person. I was worried about her. This would be her first child. One cold, snowy January night Mike came after me. Justine was in labor, and I knew it was too soon. I took the maternity box and we left.

She was having pains close together and soon a very tiny two and a half pound baby girl arrived. Then to my surprise ten minutes later a partially formed fetus appeared. The little head looked like a frog. The first fetus was alive and well-formed but so small!

Perce, Mike, and I made an incubator with hot water bottles and tried to keep the baby alive. For two days I spent most of my waking hours with Justine and the baby but it was a losing battle. After doing everything I could possibly do, I knew I had lost.

That wasn't my only worry: Justine was running a fever. I knew some of the placenta was still in the uterus. I had given her penicillan but to no avail. I knew that uremia had set in and Justine would die if I didn't get her to the hospital.

At once I sent a dog team to Hamilton with a wire for a plane to pick up Justine and fly her to Mountain Village Hospital. We waited several hours, but no plane came. While we were listening to the short wave radio, we heard Claude Hirst, my boss, saying, "If Starritt says she needs a plane, she needs a plane. Get one down there immediately!"

After two hours the plane arrived. Perce and Mike carried Justine and put her in the plane. On take-off the plane hit rough ice and broke a ski. Justine was terrified. Mike and Perce brought her back to the schoolhouse. The pilot wired for another plane.

Now I was frightened. It was taking so long for transportation to arrive that she might die on the way to the hospital. When the second plane landed, Justine was fighting, not wanting to get aboard; but Mike carried her and forced her to go. The plane was in time and her life was saved.

She later realized that if she had not flown to the hospital she would not have survived. In appreciation, she made me a tiny pair of sealskin water boots and told me in Eskimo how grateful she was to me for saving her life. I still have the tiny water boots.

Spring of 1941 was as usual: teaching, taking care of the village problems and the sick. We decided to take a vacation. We hadn't been home since we had arrived in Alaska in October, 1936. I closed school the second week in March. Everyone in the village was leaving to hunt muskrat.

From Alex Okitkun, at Williams Trading Post, I had bought the two best red fox furs that had been brought to the trading post that winter. I had sent them to New York to be made up and they had been returned. They were gorgeous, a bit flashy, but beautiful. Also I had ordered a new wool suit so I would be all dressed up in my best bib and tucker for our trip home.

We left Chaneliak on March nineteenth by dog team for Hamilton and stayed with George for three nights until the mail plane arrived from Mountain Village and flew us to Unalakeet where we stayed with Henry and Gladys.

The weather was terrible; it was the twenty-fifth of March when the twenty-four place plane could finally land and take us to Anchorage. As it had snowed heavily at Unalakeet the day before, we were dressed in parkas and mukluks. When we got on the plane, there was only one passenger, a salesman. For a month, air travel had been hazardous, so few people were flying. When we reached Rainy Pass it was snowing so heavily we couldn't see the wing tips of the plane. The air currents were rough; we were bouncing up and down and from side to side. We had flown many times, but this was the first time I was frightened. I was thinking maybe this would be our last flight!

These two pilots had gone through the pass many times. They put the plane on instuments and started through. Halfway was a weather station and you could see part of it. It seemed we were almost touching the edge of the mountains, we were so close. Finally the mountains disappeared and we were flying only a few yards above the bushes.

The sky had cleared; the plane climbed up into the sky; we were a few miles from Anchorage. We gave a sigh of relief. As we circled the field at Anchorage, I looked down and saw dozens of brightly painted small planes; they reminded me of butterflies huddled together.

A small bus drove us to the hotel. There was no snow, and here we were in parka and boots. I felt ridiculous. We stayed in Anchorage two days to attend to business and shop; then we took the train to Seward. The ride was spectacular, with the train traveling over high tressels, then slowly winding its way through the lush vegetation of forests. At Seward we boarded the steamer for Seattle.

After leaving Seward, we crossed the Gulf of Alaska, entered Icy Strait, and went up Lynn Canal to Haines and Skagway to take on passengers, but there was no time for us to disembark and visit Haines.

From the deck of the ship we could see many barracks and at the wharf, dozens of fishing boats. At Skagway the tall rock cliff at the wharf had hundreds of names painted and carved on it from the gold rush days of the 1890's. From Skagway we cruised down Lynn Canal, past the Mendenhall Glacier where large chunks of ice were breaking off into the canal.

As the sun was setting we docked at Juneau. Here we would stay for two days. We had reports to deliver and plans to discuss with our boss at the Juneau office. We had called friends who lived in Douglas to meet us for the day.

Douglas was reached by a bridge from Juneau, and was surrounded by flat green fields and a dairy that supplied milk to Juneau. Juneau is very different. It is built against a precipitous hillside, with steep stairways leading to many of the houses. Our friend, Dr. Rude, lived in one of these houses, with a bay window which faced the waterfall that tumbled down Gold Creek with great sprays of water and traveled on into Gastineau Channel.

We left Juneau in the middle of the night to dock at

Petersburg at three in the morning. There on the dock was our banker, Ed Locken, and his wife, waiting for us with money and checks for our trip. Not many bankers would get up at 3:00 a.m. and meet the boat to give you money, but the Lockens were exceptional people, old-timers who loved Alaska as well as the people who lived there.

We cruised down the inside passage to Wrangell and Ketchikan, across Queen Charlotte Sound and debarked at Seattle where we took the train to Oakland, and the ferry to San Francisco. At the ferry building, Dad and Mother met us. What a happy reunion! For three months we lived in another world.

After our vacation, on July second, we boarded the steamer *Columbia* at Seattle, destination Nome and Saint Michael. The ship was crowded with defense workers bound for Kodiak, Unalaska and Dutch Harbor. On board there were some personnel like ourselves, teachers and nurses working for the Office of Indian Affairs, going to Point Barrow and other villages along the route. A few were residents of Alaska, but there were no tourists.

Perce got acquainted with one of the engineers for the underground defenses at Unalaska and Dutch Harbor. This man had a drinking problem. His buddies on board were no help; so he asked Perce if he could hide in our stateroom during the day, where he would be safe from partying and drinking. We were happy to help. He and Perce played cribbage all day and half the night.

When we docked at Kodiak, many defense workers debarked. No other passengers were allowed on shore. The engineer got off on offical business; when he returned he told us that this was a critical time. It wouldn't be long before we would be in World War II.

In a few hours we were docking at Unalaska. All the remaining defense workers, including our friend, got off the boat. Those of us that were left were standing at the railing wishing we could go ashore, when a Jeep came on to the dock with our engineer friend driving. Over the loud speaker came the request that the Starritts go ashore.

I was standing beside a nurse from New York who was going to Barrow. "Westerners are so crude," she complained. "They have no manners and are uncouth. How do they get to go ashore?" I laughed and didn't bother to answer her.

Perce and I made a quick exit via the gangplank and got in the Jeep. We had two hours while the ship was being unloaded. That was enough time to see Unalaska's and Dutch Harbor's defenses. An airport was being constructed. It led into a huge underground hangar in the mountainside. Not only were the planes underground, but all the communication equipment as well. There were barracks and family homes above ground but many more living quarters were being dug into the hillside.

By the time we returned to the ship, it was time to sail into the Bering Sea. We were out to sea only a few minutes when two American planes began to circle the ship. Then to our surprise we saw two large floating canneries flying the Japanese flag. A large rising sun was painted on one side of each boat. Several small dories filled with nets were around the cannery boat. I got out my camera and took pictures of the boats. I thought it strange to have them so close to our shores. The planes stayed with us all the way to Nome.

After reaching Nome, we were told that a submarine had been sighted in the Bering Sea. That was the reason for our escort. Perce got off at Nome to go to work and I went on to Saint Michael. The *Ensee* was loaded and ready to travel up the Yukon so I got aboard, disembarked at Chaneliak for the dory, packed it with school supplies and motored up the river to Hamilton, where I picked up one of the natives to navigate down the south mouth to Kwiguk.

Once the men set up the tents, school was in session. I made the rounds of all the homes and tents but many families were at fish camps. In a week when they returned, I had thirty children. We had meetings on health care, games and plays every night. This summer I was alone, doing Alma's job as well as teaching.

By this time the children spoke some English, understood it and could read and print short sentences. For me it was very satisfying to see how the children had advanced in their lessons with so little time in school each summer.

Six weeks had passed. It was time to pack the *Loon* and travel back to Chaneliak. On the way I stopped at Hamilton to make out reports and to mail them to the Juneau office. While I was at Hamilton, George suggested we take the high-powered motor boat and go up the slew, duck and goose hunting. It sounded like fun so I agreed.

George and I started up the Yukon and soon turned into one of the larger slews. The sky was overcast and a brisk wind was blowing the mosquitoes away. We went into many more slews, shut off the motor and waited. Before long, a flock of geese would land and George would kill one or two. Then he would wade out in his hip boots and gather the kill.

While we were cruising through the slews, George at the wheel, I looked around at the vast wild country wondering how the first Eskimos settled in such a place. Then I saw a red fox running along a small beach watching us, curious as to what we were doing invading his privacy. Further on we saw a pair of white swans gliding along in the water with three cygnets paddling fast to keep up with their parents. How lovely they were! One wonders how anyone can harm them.

George guided the boat into a slew that was so narrow I thought we were cruising on the grass. He shut off the motor and we waited. Soon a flock of snow geese came overhead to land a few yards away. George, still sitting so as not to disturb the birds, raised the shotgun and pulled the trigger. The gun made a strange noise and the barrel blew apart, knocking him over in the boat. I screamed, the geese flew and I said, "Oh! My God, what has happened?"

Stunned, I was thinking, "We will never get out of here." I had no notion which direction to take. About this time, he regained his senses. He didn't seem injured, only shaken. He said, "Can you run this boat? I can guide you back to the river. I feel a bit ill." I told him I would try, and could manage if he gave me directions. Starting the motor, I very slowly guided the boat out of the narrow slew to where the channel widened. With George directing me and not too much speed, I finally made our way back to the Yukon and Hamilton. I was never so grateful in my life as when I docked that boat, with the knowledge that George was not injured.

Waska was at Hamilton to help me home with the *Loon.* On our way down the Yukon, flocks of geese were flying in large formations, getting ready for their long trip south. Waska had his twenty-two and would stop now and then to shoot at a duck or a goose.

About half-way home we saw a flock of strange large birds flying overhead. They landed a few yards from the river on a little lake. Beaching the Loon, Waska started toward the lake with his gun. Soon there was a shot. He returned with one of the strange birds. It looked like a penguin with a large wing spread. Neither Waska nor anyone else in the village had seen such a bird. We thought they might have come from the Canadian side and, because of bad weather, been thrown off their regular beaten path.

When we arrived home, Perce had returned from Nome and Father from Stebbins. Father was worried about Mike, who lived at Pastolik. He and Mary, his wife, were not getting along. Father hired Alex's boat, the Daisy, to go to Pastolik, asking Perce to accompany him. Perce consented. When they arrived at Pastolik, Mike and Mary were shouting at each other.

"You are a bad husband. You are lazy and do not hunt," Mary said.

"You are a scolding, disagreeable wife. I do not want to live with you any longer," Mike replied.

Father and Perce had soon listened to their quarreling long enough; so Perce interrupted the bickering and said, "Mike, if you and Mary can't get along, you just move out."

Mary agreed that she didn't want him around. Mike said, "I will be happy to leave." He gathered up his reindeer sleeping bag, a blanket, a tin cup, his gun, his six dogs and sled, all his worldly possessions, and put them on the boat.

He was divorced. Afterwards, Perce always enjoyed telling the story of how he divorced Mike and Mary. Divorces among the Eskimos were easy and informal. If there were children, they stayed with their mother. In Mike's case, there were no children. He remained at Chaneliak until freezeup, then, with his dog team, went to live upriver.

In the winter of forty-one, the war news worsened. On December 7, we heard on the radio that the Japanese had bombed Pearl Harbor in Hawaii. We told our native friends but it was of little concern to them. Waska said to Perce, "Maybe they be better to us, we get more." Perce was really upset by such a remark and replied, "Yes, they will probably drop a bomb on Chaneliak, blow you up and that will be the end of you."

After the bombing of Pearl Harbor, Japanese reconnaissance planes flew over Nome at the precise same time every day, but never dropped bombs. We were frightened. After coming back in July and knowing we had so little defense, we thought the Japanese might take Dutch Harbor, and we would be under Japanese occupation. Actually, although they bombed the harbor and Unalaska, they landed only on the island at the end of the Aleutian chain. The teachers we had traveled with on the *North Star* were taken as prisoners to Japan. They would be released at the end of the war, unharmed.

Perce and I had been at Chaneliak five years, improved living conditions, and taken care of health problems. With conditions so unsettled, we decided to ask for a transfer to the Bethel area, where we wouldn't be so isolated.

At that time, we heard that the trading post and boarding house were for sale, and we were considering changing profession. The Juneau office approved our transfer to Akiachak on the Kuskokwim River and we accepted.

Then began the packing, cleaning and putting everything in order for the next teachers. Muskrat season arrived. A few natives left the village, but most stayed until break-up which was early. We were ready and waiting for the *Ensee's* first trip of the season upriver. Captain Holsher sent a deck hand in a large dory for us and our gear.

The entire village, including Father, were at the schoolhouse to say farewells. Everyone seemed sad, even Keoria, the medicine man. He brought me a gift, two old slate knives, *ulus*, that the Eskimos had used before the arrival of the whalers, and a wooden mask that he had used in his medicine making. After many handshakes, we were off, never to see our Eskimo friends again.

As soon as the deck hands had loaded our belongings on the *Ensee*, we were on our way upriver. Thousands of birds were returning to nest. Ducks, geese, seagulls and arctic terns were flying overhead. Snipes were running along the shores and two sand cranes were feeding, while two loons were swimming in the middle of the river. The wind was blowing and white puffy clouds were showing their heads in the blue sky.

We stopped at Hamilton and, while the freight for the trading post was being unloaded, we said our goodbyes to George. He had been a good and helpful friend for five years. Leaving Hamilton, we proceded up the wide mucky Yukon for several hours to reach Mountain Village. While the freight was being unloaded, we went up to the small hospital and told the doctor we had left Chaneliak. After being shown around the hospital, we were treated to lunch. Back on board the *Ensee,* we continued upriver, stopping at Andreafsky and Pilot Station, but we didn't get off the boat. There were only a few cabins and a store at each place.

It wasn't long before we reached Marshall, also called Fortuna Ledge. Stuart Widener and Kathryn, his wife, were waiting at the dock for us. We had become friends, traveling together on the *North Star* when we first came to Chaneliak. Stuart was now deputy marshal for the Territory of Alaska, stationed at Fortuna Ledge. We were to stay with them until Nat Brown, the bush pilot, came to fly us to Akiachak. A week passed and no Nat Brown. He sent word that he had to take off the skis and put the pontoons on his plane.

Ours turned out to be a long wait. Perce got acquainted with Louie, the storekeeper. He was so busy with all the Eskimos bringing in their dried muskrat skins that he didn't take time to sleep. The store was open twenty-four hours a day. He sat at the counter counting the skins, entering the Eskimos' credit in his account book. Sitting in the same spot, he would fall asleep, wake up and continue writing where he had left off, without moving a muscle except to write.

With their credit for the skins, the Eskimos would begin their shopping by selecting one thing at a time and bringing the article up to Louie, who would record it in the ledger. Slowly, they would start looking for something else. This procedure would go on all day, into the night and on to the next day. The Eskimo shop-keeper needed patience and Louie, who had been at Fortuna Ledge for many years, had the patience. It was his livelihood.

Louie needed help; so Perce went to work in the warehouse, counting twenty muskrat skins to a bundle and tagging them for shipment to Seattle. While Perce was helping Louie, I talked to the people living at the rooming house.

Late one night, one of the men from the rooming house awakened us by pounding on the Wideners' door.

When Stuart opened the door, the man said, "My wife has had a miscarriage. Would Mrs. Starritt come and help us?" I dressed and immediately went with him. Other friends were there making her comfortable. The wife had had a miscarriage before. She was crying and upset; so I gave her medicine to help her sleep. She was continuing to bleed: I didn't think it was a good sign. When she began to run a fever, I knew something was wrong. Penicillin failed to bring the fever down. After the second day, I suggested to her husband that he send her to the Bethel Hospital, less than an hour's flying time away. They didn't want to do this, and thought that I was premature, that she would get better. I tried to explain the seriousness of her condition. They didn't heed the warning.

Her condition became worse until, after a week, they sent for the plane. I was afraid it was too late. On her first day in the hospital, she died. I was so sorry; but I had no jurisdiction and could not force her to go as we had done with Justine at Chaneliak. I thought I should have done more. I had tried, but I failed to make them understand.

One month went by. Every day seemed a year. The war news was worse. Stuart and Kathryn had three children; a son, Gordon, six years old, a three-year old daughter, and a baby boy. Kathryn was beside herself. She wanted to take the children home to Virginia but could not handle them alone. It seemed as if Nat Brown was never coming for us; so one morning, when we heard the Japanese had invaded Attu and taken the teachers as prisoners to Japan, Perce and I decided maybe we should leave Alaska and help Kathryn with the children. Kathryn was delighted.

We wired the Juneau office and resigned. George Butler heard the message to Juneau and immediately talked to Perce on Louie's short wave radio. He insisted we were crazy to leave Alaska and we would regret it, that we should reconsider; but we had made a commitment to the Wideners.

We sent to Nome for a four-place plane to fly us to Fairbanks. Leaving all our Eskimo boots and parkas with Stuart, we told him to give them to a native who would make good use of them.

One quiet, sunny morning with no wind, few clouds

and millions of mosquitoes, the little plane landed at Marshall. Kathryn would care for the baby, I the little girl, and Perce would care for Gordon, the six-year-old. Friends were there to see us off. We climbed aboard the plane and flew up into the clear, blue sky, past Holy Cross and the Yukon, Mosquito Mountain, and Beaver Mountain, over rivers and small lakes, then landed for gas at McGrath. The mosquitoes were thick on the windshield. The pilot advised us not to get out of the plane or we would be eaten alive. We took his advice.

From McGrath, we flew along the north fork of the Kuskokwim River, the Kuskokwim Mountains on the north side of us and Mt. McKinley on the south. Mt. McKinley was pushed up many millions of years ago, the tallest mountain in North America. It looked like a cathedral, covered with snow and surrounded by many peaks poking their heads above scattered clouds. The Indians called it *Denali*, the Great One. Lower on the slopes, forests grew. Below us were numerous rivers and lakes. We flew over enormous bluegreen Lake Minchumina, with thousands of water birds on the surface.

Now we were approaching Fairbanks. As we neared the airport, the pilot was informed he couldn't get clearance to land as the military had permission to land before us. Dusk was coming on while we circled the field for over half an hour. Gas was running low. By this time we were all very nervous. Finally, we got permission to land.

We were a happy crew to step on the good old earth again. Not knowing when we would get passage to Seattle, we took a taxi to the hotel. The military and defense workers were being flown to Fairbanks and other points in Alaska before any civilians could get passage. When we went to get our tickets at the Wien Airlines, we were told that, if there was any space on any plane, they would give us twenty minutes notice to get to the airport, which was over seven miles away. We kept our bags packed while we waited. Over a week passed and no flight.

Perce was offered several jobs with construction firms: Fort Wainright and the Yukon Command Training Site were being built. We liked Alaska and wanted to stay, but we had made a commitment. We didn't feel we could leave Kathryn and the children stranded at Fairbanks. This changed our whole lives, and I still wonder what life would have been like if we had stayed at Fairbanks.

After two miserable weeks of waiting, not able to leave the hotel for any length of time, we received a call at 10:00 p.m., to inform us that there was space on a twenty-seat plane leaving in twenty minutes. We each grabbed our luggage and a child and off we went in the pouring rain. When we reached the airport, we had three minutes to board. Because of war time, everything was blacked out.

The children had their throwing-up bags. They were always air sick, but they had flown so many times, it didn't bother them. I remembered that Kathryn was in her cabin almost the entire trip on the *North Star* because she was seasick; it must have run in the family. There was no help, no stewardess on this flight, everyone on his own. The storm was intensifying. One couldn't see anything but dark clouds, flashes of lightning and sheets of rain. The pilots decided to land at Douglas, where we would be bussed across the bridge to Juneau. The plane company put us up at the Baranoff Hotel.

Weather the next day was no better. Perce and I went to the Juneau office to say our goodbyes. It was a sad meeting for everyone, including Claude, my boss. Tears came to my eyes. It had been a good working relationship and I wanted to stay, but it wasn't meant to be.

We flew out the next day in fair weather. Landing at Prince George for gas, no one was allowed off the plane. Leaving Prince George, we flew down Fraser River. On both sides of the river were mountains covered with dense forests. When we flew over Vancouver, six-year-old Gordon, looking out the window, exclaimed, "Boy! What a big village!" He had never seen large cities, only Alaskan villages.

In no time at all, the shades were pulled down in the plane, and we were landing in Seattle. When my luggage went through customs, officials found the slides I had taken of the Japanese cannery ships in Bristol Bay on our trip back to Alaska in July, 1941. We were detained to explain the slides, but only for a short time. They took our names and addresses, and returned the slides. Here we were back in the lower forty-eight states, never to return to Alaska again.

Eskimo Legends

Introduction:

Story telling was an important part of Eskimo life. In the *Kashim,** men told legends and illustrated them by drawing on the dirt floor, sometimes using a story knife made of ivory. Eskimo dances, too, told stories. Some acted out the old folk tales. Others represented the hunting and travel adventures of the story tellers.

Usually each story carried a lesson. Parents and grand-parents taught the children through these folk tales. So it was not surprising that one of the favorite activities of the pupils was writing down and illustrating the ancient legends.

Porcupine

Porcupine was an old woman who lived at the end of the village. She liked the people there and decided to give them berries in the *kashim*. When she went to the *kashim*, she first danced, then she sang.

While she was singing and dancing, she heard someone say, "Porcupine has a funny nose. It is so long."

This made Porcupine angry and unhappy, so she took her berries and went home. Porcupine thought the people hated her, and since they were unkind, she would not give them anything. She worked hard and was so busy that she forgot her neighbors and their unkindness.

Note: We should not say unkind words about anyone.

* **Kashim: A gathering place, used mostly by the men and boys of the village.**

The Elf Man

The Elf Man awoke. He sat up and looked around. He was in a very large *kashim* with a wide bench running all around the walls. He had been lying under the open sky-light.

Speaking aloud his thoughts, he said, "How did I come here? Where did I come from? Where are the great medicine men? Perhaps they could help me." Looking at the benches, he spoke again, "To which of these benches shall I go?"

He stood up. Turning to the left, he climbed upon the bench and looked around. He saw a fingernail.

"So humans have passed this way."

Seeing the door, he jumped down from the bench and went out. He found he was on a high knoll. He walked around the *kashim*, which was a human skull partly buried in the moss. One eye was the door. The base of the skull was the sky-light. When he was inside, he thought he was a very big man. Now, as he stood beside it, he knew that he was very tiny.

"Fairies must have brought me here when I was asleep. I shall live here and this skull will be my home. I will go to sleep again."

He went into the *kashim* and fell asleep. He slept for many hundreds of years. The fairies had changed him from a real man to an elf.

Note: Even now, hunters on the tundra near Pikmitalik see dwarf people. If someone tries to get close, the dwarf suddenly disappears into the ground.

Friendly Bear

Once an old brown bear lived on the mountain side by himself. It was summertime in the moon of the blueberries. One day, the wind was calm and the sun was hot. The bear went to the other side of the mountain to find blueberries. When he reached the berry patch, he began to eat. After awhile he heard someone singing behind him. He looked around to see who it was, but he saw nothing. He began to eat again; then he heard someone singing as before. He looked everywhere but saw nothing. The bear turned to the blueberries and ate and ate. The third time he heard the singing, he turned and saw a red poll perched on the low branches of a bush.

Brown Bear said, "Come and eat blueberries with me and have some fun."

The red poll flew to the bear and ate berries.

While they were eating, Bear said, "Let me paint your head with blueberry juice. When it dries, it will be red, and as long as you live, some of your feathers shall be colored with red."

The red poll answered, "I would like to have my head painted; then I will be beautiful."

The bear took a blueberry and crushed it in his huge paw; then he painted the little grey bird on the top of the head. They let it dry in the hot sun. When it was dry, the little bird showed it to the bear.

The bear said, "It is very, very nice."

After he had thanked the bear, the red poll flew away.

Note: That is why red polls have red on their heads.